HANOVER; OR THE PERSECUTION OF THE LOWLY A STORY OF THE WILMINGTON MASSACRE • THORNE, JACK

end of this book .... 47. All other inconsistencies are as in the original. The author's spelling has been retained.

HANOVER; OR THE PERSECUTION OF THE LOWLY.

A Story of the Wilmington Massacre

BY
JACK THORNE

Published by M. C. L. Hill.
Respectfully dedicated to
the eminent heroine
Ida B. Wells Barnett

Negroes Fleeing From Wilmington. 1
Introductory Note. 2
CHAPTER I. 4
CHAPTER II. 5
CHAPTER III. 8
CHAPTER IV. 10
CHAPTER V. 12
CHAPTER VI. 15
CHAPTER VII. 17
CHAPTER VIII. 19
CHAPTER IX. 21
CHAPTER X. 23
CHAPTER XI. 24
CHAPTER XII. 26
CHAPTER XIII. 31
CHAPTER XIV. 33
CHAPTER XV. 36
CHAPTER XVI. 37
CHAPTER XVII. 37
CHAPTER XVIII. 41
CHAPTER XIX. 43
CHAPTER XX. 43
CHAPTER XXI. 44
CHAPTER XXII. 45
CHAPTER XXIII. 46
Molly's Final Step. 46

Publisher's Note

Purchase of this book entitles you to a free trial membership in the publisher's book club at www.rarebooksclub.com. (Time limited offer.) Simply enter the barcode number from the back cover onto the membership form on our home page. The book club entitles you to select from millions of books at no additional charge. You can also download a digital copy of this and related books to read on the go. Simply enter the title or subject onto the search form to find them.

Note: This is an historic book. Pages numbers, where present in the text, refer to the first edition of the book and may also be in indexes.

If you have any questions, could you please be so kind as to consult our Frequently Asked Questions page at www.rarebooksclub.com/faqs.cfm? You are also welcome to contact us there.

Publisher: Books LLC™, Memphis, TN, USA, 2012. ISBN: 9781153810401.

Proofreading: pgdp.net

Transcriber's note

A Table of Contents has been created for this version.

Minor punctuation errors have been corrected without notice. Printer's errors have been corrected, and they are indicated with a
mouse-hover 47
and listed at the
[3]

NEGROES FLEEING FROM WILMINGTON.

Driven out by Organized Bands of "Red Shirts." Obnoxious White Men Also Ordered to get out of Town. No Lynching Allowed. Mayor Waddell and his Police Prevent Further Killing. Rule of Whites now Prevail. Three Hundred Policemen Sworn in to Preserve Order—No Collision Between the Races Expected. No Trade at Wilmington.
[Associated Press Market Report]

Wilmington, N. C., Nov. 11. —Spirits turpentine—Nothing doing.

Rosin—Nothing doing.

Crude turpentine—Nothing doing.

Wilmington, Nov. 11. —With the killing of the Negroes yesterday the backbone of the trouble seems to have been broken. The authors of the tragedy have gone to their homes and the mob has disbanded as if in contempt of the gangs of Negroes who still hang about in the black quarters growling and threatening the whites.

Law and order are gradually being restored; and those among the Negroes who feel resentment against the whites are afraid to show their true colors.

Early this morning 300 resolute white men gathered at the Mayor's office and were sworn in as new policemen.

Late last night half a hundred white citizens got together and planned a big lynching party which was to raid the city from centre to circumference today.

There were six Negroes in jail who had been arrested during the excitement of the day, and who some people of the town thought should be summarily dispatched. One was a leader, Thomas Miller, who was charged with declaring that he would wash his hands in a white man's blood before night. Another was A. R. Bryant, charged with being a dangerous character; the others were less prominent, but had been under the ban of the whites for conduct calculated to incite trouble.

Mayor Waddell and his associates put a veto upon the proposed lynching. [4] They said that good government was to prevail in Wilmington from this time, and would commence immediately. The would-be lynchers were so insistent that the Mayor called out a guard and kept the jail surrounded all night.

This morning the six Negroes were taken out and escorted to the north bound train by a detachment of militia, to be banished from the city. The citizens cheered as they saw them going, for they considered their departure conducive to peace in the future.

G. Z. French, one of the county leaders, attempted to escape. He ran through the streets, but was overtaken at the depot by several members of the posse.

A noose was thrown over his head and was drawn tightly around his neck. Gasping and half choked, he fell upon his knees, begging for his life.

NEGRO BEGS FOR LIFE.

"Do you solemnly promise that you will leave and never come back?" asked the leader of the posse.

"Oh, yes; yes. For God's sake, gentlemen, let me go, and I'll never come back any more!"

The frightened wretch was allowed to go and crawled aboard the train, scared half to death.

After finishing with French the "red shirts" made a raid on Justice Bunting's residence. He was away from home. The mob tore from the walls of his house the picture of his Negro wife and that of Bunting, and put them on exhibition on Market street.

They were labelled: "R. H. Bunting, white," and "Mrs. R. H. Bunting, colored." From Bunting's residence the mob proceeded to the house of a Negro lawyer named Henderson. The hard-knuckled leader knocked at the door. "Who's .... 47 there?" came the query. "A white man and a friend," was the reply. Inside there was the deep silence of hesitation. "Open the door or we'll break it down," shouted the leader. Henderson, badly frightened, opened the door.

"We want you to leave the city by 9 o'clock Sunday morning," said the leader.

"All right," replied Henderson, "all I want is time enough to get my things in order."

A Negro lawyer named Scott was also banished and left the city before morning.

The Democrats hired one of Pinkerton's Negro detectives to associate with the Negroes several weeks, and his investigation, it is said, revealed that the two lawyers and the other Negroes mentioned were ringleaders, who were inciting their race to violence. [5]

WHITE MEN MUST GO TOO.

The retiring chief of police, Magistrate R. H. Bunting, Charles H. Gilbert, Charles McAlister, all white Republicans, and many assertive Negroes, who are considered dangerous to the peace of the community, are now under guard and are to be banished from the city.

The Negro Carter Peaman, who was exiled last night, got off the train several miles from the city and was shot dead.

A report is current that John C. Dancy, the Negro United States Collector of Customs for this port, has been notified to leave the city and will be waited upon if orders are not summarily obeyed.

The city is now under thorough military and police protection and there is no indication of further outbreaks.

[6]

Introductory Note.

On the Cape Fear River, about thirty miles from the East coast of North Carolina rests the beautiful city of Wilmington.

Wilmington is the metropolis; the most important city of the old North State, and in fact, is one of the chief seaports of the Atlantic coast. The city lies on the East bank of the river, extending mainly Northward and Southward. Market Street, the centre and main thoroughfare of the city, wide and beautiful, begins at the river front and gradually climbs a hill Eastward, so persistently straight, that the first rays of a Summer's morning sun kiss the profusion of oak and cedar trees that border it; and the evening sun seems to linger in the Western heavens, loath to bid adieu to that foliage-covered crest.

Wilmington is the Mecca for North Carolina's interior inhabitants who flock thither to breathe in its life-giving ocean breezes when Summer's torrid air becomes unbearable, and lazy Lawrence dances bewilderingly before the eyes. The Winter climate is temperate, but not congenial to Northern tourists, who like swallows, only alight there for a brief rest, and to look around on their journeying to and from the far South: yet Wilmington is cosmopolitan; There dwells the thrifty Yankee, the prosperous Jew, the patient and docile Negro, the enterprising, cunning and scrupulous German; and among her first families are the Scotch-Irish, descendants of the survivors of Culloden. Wilmington suckled children who rallied under Scott in Mexico, heard the thunderings at Monterey, and the immortal Alamo. When the civil strife of four years was nearing its close, when the enemies to the Union of States, sullen and vindictive, were retreating before an invading army, Wilmington, nestling behind Fort Fisher, one of the most formidable fortresses ever contrived, was shaken by some of the most terrific bombarding that ever took place on earth.

"Then thronged the citizens with terror dumb

Or Whispering with white lips, 'The foe! they come! they come!'"

Wilmington, the scene of one of the last desperate stands of a demoralized army, witnessed the "memorizing of Golgotha" as her sons desperately struggled to resist a conquering foe. In Oak Dale Cemetery on the Northeastern boundary of the city sleep a few of the [7] principal actors in that tragedy. There rests noble James; there rests Colonel Hall— grand old Roman! I am glad he did not live to see the 10th of November, 1898, lest he should have been tempted to join that mob of misguided citizens whose deeds of cowardice plunged that city, noted for its equity, into an abyss of infamy. Southward from Oak Dale Cemetery awaiting the final reveille, are calmly sleeping not a few of that Grand Army who fell in the arms of victory at Fort Fisher.

During the slave period, North Carolina could not be classed with South Carolina, Georgia, and other far Southern States in cruelty and inhumanity to its slave population; and in Wilmington and vicinity, the pillage of a victorious army, and the Reconstruction period were borne with resignation. Former master and freedman vied with each other in bringing order out of chaos, building up waste places, and recovering lost fortunes. Up to but a few years ago, the best feeling among the races prevailed in Wilmington; the Negro and his white brother walked their beats together on the police force; white and black aldermen, white mayor and black chief of police, white and black school committeemen sat together in council; white and black mechanics worked together on the same buildings, and at the same bench; white and black teachers taught in the same schools. Preachers, lawyers and physicians were cordial in their greetings one toward the other, and general good-feeling prevailed. Negroes worked, saved, bought lands and built houses. Old wooden meeting houses were torn down, and handsome brick churches went up in their places. Let the prejudiced scoffer say what he will, the Negro has done his full share in making the now illfated city blossom as the rose. We who have for so many years made our abode elsewhere, have made our boast in Wilmington as being ahead of all other Southern cities in the recognition of the citizenship of all of her inhabitants; unstained by such acts of violence that had disgraced other communities. To be laid to rest 'neath North Carolina pines has been the wish of nearly every pilgrim who has left that dear old home. All this is changed now; That old city is no longer dear. The spoiler is among the works of God. Since the massacre on the 10th of November, 1898, over one thousand of Wilmington's most respected taxpaying citizens have sold and given away their belongings, and like Lot fleeing from Sodom, have hastened away. The lawyer left his client, the physician his patients, the carpenter his work-bench, the shoemaker his tools—all have fled, fled for their lives; fled to escape murder and pillage, intimidation and insult at hands of a bloodthirsty mob of ignorant descendants of England's indentured slaves, fanned into frenzy by their more intelligent leaders [8] whose murderous schemes to obtain office worked charmingly. Legally elected officers have been driven from the city which is now ruled by a banditti whose safety in office is now threatened by the disappointed poor whites whose aid was secured in driving out wealthy Negroes on the promise that the Negroes' property should be turned over to them.

What has wrought all this havoc in the city once so peaceful? Rev. A. J. McKelway of Charlotte, Editor of the *North Carolina Presbyterian*, in an article published in the *New York Independent* of November, 1898, explains as follows:—"In 1897 was passed at Governor Russell's wish and over the protest of the Western Republicans, a bill to amend the charter of the city. If there had been any condition of bad or inefficient government, there might have been some excuse for this action; but the city was admirably governed by those who were most interested in her growth and welfare. Here is the law that is responsible for the bloodshed recently in Wilmington:"

" Be it Enacted, That there shall be elected by the qualified voters of each ward one Alderman only, and there shall be appointed by the Governor one Alderman for each ward, and the Board of Aldermen thus constituted shall elect a Mayor according to the laws declared to be in force by this act."

"It will be readily seen that, combining with those elected from the Negro wards, it was easy for the appointees of the Governor to elect the Mayor and appoint the other city officers."

"When the new Board took possession there were found to be three Aldermen, fourteen policemen, seventeen officers in the fire department, four deputy sheriffs, and forty Negro magistrates besides. It is probable that *not one of these* was qualified to fill his office. The new government soon found itself incapable of governing. It could not control its own. The homes of the people were at the mercy of thieves, burglars and incendiaries, and the police were either absolutely incapable of preventing crime, or connived at it. White women were insulted on the streets in broad daylight by Negro men, and on more than one occasion slapped in the face by Negro women on no provocation. * * * * White people began to arm themselves for the protection of their lives and property. * * * * In the city of Wilmington it has been found upon investigation, that the Negroes own 5 per cent. of the property, and pay 5 per cent. of the taxes. * * *

"The Negro editor publicly charged to the white women of the South equal blame for the unspeakable crime, etc."

The Rev. Mr. McKelway has worded his defense well; but in giving a plausible excuse for the crime of Nov. 10th, he makes a dismal [9] failure. A mob headed by a minister of the gospel, and a hoary-headed deacon, after cutting off every avenue of escape and defense, and after the government had been surrendered to them as a peace offering, wantonly kills and butchers their brethren, is without parallel in a Christian community, and the more Mr. McKelway seeks to excuse such a deed, the blacker it appears.

The Hon. Judson Lyon, Register of the United States Treasury, in his reply to Senator McLaurin in the *New York Herald*, says truthfully: "In Wilmington, N. C., albeit the Executive as a leader of his party had backed down and surrendered everything as a peace offering, and the democracy, if that is what they call themselves, had carried the day, still the main thoroughfares of that city were choked with armed men. They destroyed personal property, they burned houses, they wantonly took more than a dozen lives, they drove thousands to the woods where nearly a dozen infants were born and died in many instances, with their mothers the victims of exposure as the result of the cruelty of people who call themselves democrats and patriots. Weyler in his maddest moments was hardly more barbarous."

In the city of Wilmington, where so much innocent blood had been spilled and so many valuable lives had been taken by that furious mob, see what are the facts:

There were ten members of the Board of Aldermen, seven of these white and three colored; there were twenty-six policemen, sixteen white and ten colored, the chief being white and a native of the State, city Attorney a white Republican, city clerk and treasurer, white, with colored clerk. Turnkeys and janitors white Republicans with colored assistants, Superintendent of Streets a white man, Superintendent of garbage carts a white man, Clerk of Front Street Market, a white man, Clerk of Fourth Street Market, a white man, Superintendent of Health, a white Democrat, two lot inspectors, colored men, Chief of Fire Department and Assistant chief, both white Democrats. There are three white fire companies and two colored. Superintendent of City Hospital is a white Democrat with white nurses for white wards, and colored nurses for colored wards. The school committees have always had two white members and one colored. Superintendent of Public Schools is a white Democrat.

Now, will somebody point out where that awful thing that is iterated and reiterated so much, to wit, NEGRO DOMINATION existed under this showing in the communicipality of Wilmington.

The men who were driven from the city by the mob, with but few exceptions, had no political following, nor political aspirations.

[10] It has always been the rule with mobs to villify their victims, assail their characters in the most shameful manner in justification of their murder. But an attack upon the character and integrity of the Negroes of Wilmington, in order to justify the massacre of Nov. 10th, shall not go unchallenged. If what I write should raise a howl of protest and call another ex-Governor Northern to Boston to brand it as a lie, it is nevertheless a truthful statement of the causes that led up to the doings of the 10th of November, and although I shall fictitiously name some of the star actors in this tragedy and the shifters of the scenes, I can call them all by their names and point them out. It will be proven that the massacre of Nov. 10th, 1898, had been carefully planned by the leading wealthy citizens of Wilmington, and that over thirty thousand dollars was subscribed to buy arms and ammunition to equip every man and boy of the white race, rich and poor; that secret dispatches were sent to sympathizers in adjoining States and communities to come in and assist in making the 10th of November, 1898, a second Bartholemew's eve in the history of the world, by the wholesale killing of black citizens after every means of defense had been cut off; that black men and women for banishment and slaughter had been carefully listed; that clubs and clans of assassins had been organized and drilled in signals and tactics; that the aid of the State militia and the Naval Reserves had been solicited to enter Wilmington on the 10th of November to assist in disarming every Negro, and aiding in his slaughter and banishment. That the intervention of Providence in the earnest and persistent entreaties of white citizens who were too nobly bred to stoop so low, and the strategy and cunning of the Negro himself, frustrated the carrying out to its fullest intent, one of the most infamous and cowardly deeds ever planned.

[11]

CHAPTER I.

The Editor.

"I will not retract! No! Not a single sentence! I have told the truth. This woman not satisfied with the South's bloody record since the war, is clamoring and whining like a she wolf for more human sacrifices, and an increased flow of human blood. She is unmercifully pounding a helpless and defenseless people. The article was issued in defense of the defenseless. It is right against wrong; truth against error, and it must stand even if the one who uttered it is annihilated; it must stand!"

"But you must remember my dear man, that the South is no place to speak plainly upon race matters. You have written the truth, but its a truth that the white people of the South cannot and will not stand. Now the leading whites are much incensed over this article of yours which they interpret as an intent to slander white women, and I am sent to say to you that they demand that you retract or leave the city."

"I will do neither! The truth has been said, a slanderer rebuked. God help me, I will not go back on that truth."

"Well, I leave you; I've done my duty. Good morning."

It is often said that there is nothing so indispensible as the newspaper. It is the moulder of public opinion; the medium of free speech; the promoter and stimulator of business; the prophet, the preacher, swaying the multitudes and carrying them like the whirlwind into the right or wrong path. To millions its the Bible, the Apostles Creed. Their opinion of God, of religion, of immortality is shaped by what the newspaper has to say upon such subjects. Glowing headlines in the newspapers have kindled the flames of Anarchy, and started men upon the path of destruction like wolves stimulated and brutalized by the scent of blood, to pause only when irrepairable evil [12] hath been wrought. —"When new widows howl and new orphans cry." What a power for evil is the newspaper! The newspaper arrayed on the side of the right hurls its mighty battering-ram against gigantic walls of opresion until they fall; takes up the cause of the bondman, echoes his wails and the clanking of his chains until the nation is aroused, and men are marching shoulder to shoulder on to the conflict for the right. What a power for good is the newspaper! I once heard a great editor say that "although newspaper work was hard and laborious, requiring a great store of intellectual strength it was nevertheless a fascinating work." But in the South where freedom of speech is limited to a class *grit and backbone* outweigh intellectual ability and are far more requisite. When we consider the fact that many white newspaper men have "licked the dust" in the Southland because they dared to emerge from the trend of popular thought and opinion, the Spartan who without a tremor held his hand into the flames until it had burned away was not more a subject of supreme admiration than the little Octoroon editor of the *Wilmington Record* whose brave utterances begin this chapter.

The great newspapers of today are too engrossed in weightier matters to concern themselves to any extent with things that promote directly the interests of the ten million black Americans. That is largely the cause of the existence of the Negro editors. The Negro, like the white man, likes to read something good of himself; likes to see his picture in the paper; likes to read of the social and business affairs of his people; likes to see the bright and sunnyside of his character portrayed; so he often turns from the great journals (who are if saying anything at all concerning him, worrying over the "Negro Problem" (?)) to look at the bright side presented by the Negro newspaper. A few days ago while worried and disconsolate over the aspersions heaped upon a defenseless people that floated upon the feotid air from the Alabama Conference, *The New York Age* came to me, a ray of light in a dungeon of gross darkness.

Prior to the year 1892 there had been no genuine zeal among colored people to establish a colored newspaper in Wilmington. *The Record* was launched at about that time: but not until taken in hand by the famous A. L. Manly did it amount to very much as a news me [13] dium. Under the management of this enterprising little man *The Record* forged ahead, and at the time of its suspension was the only Negro daily, perhaps, in the country. It was a strong champion of the cause of Wilmington's colored citizens. Improvements in the section of the city owned by black people were asked for, and the request granted. Good roads were secured, bicycle paths made, etc. The greatest deed achieved however, was the exposure by *The Record* of the very unsanitary condition of the colored wards in the city hospital. *The Record* made such a glowing picture of the state of affairs, that the Board of County Commissioners were compelled to investigate and take action, which resulted in the putting of the old hospital in habitable shape. This, though a good work, did not enhance the Editor's popularity with the whites who thought him too *high strung, bold and saucy*. And the colored people who appreciated his pluck felt a little shaky over his many tilts with editors of the white papers. The brave little man did not last very long however—the end came apace: Sitting in his office one evening in August reading a New York paper, his eyes fell upon a clipping from a Georgia paper from the pen of a famous Georgia white woman, whose loud cries for the lives of Negro rapists had been so very widely read and commented upon during the past year. This particular article referred to the exposure of and the protection of white girls in the isolated districts of the South from lustful brutes. "Narrow-souled fool!" exclaimed the editor, throwing the paper upon the floor; "I wonder does she ever think of the Negro girls in isolated districts of the South exposed to lustful whites! Does she think of those poor creatures shorn of all protection by the men of her race! I guess her soul is too small to be generous a little bit.—'White girls in isolated districts exposed to lustful Negro brutes.' Colored girls in isolated districts exposed to lustful white brutes; what's the difference? Does the Negro's ruined home amount to nought? Can man sin against his neighbor without suffering its consequences? 'Woe unto you Scribes and Pharisees, hypocrites!' I'll throw a broadside at that old women, so help me God."

The editor took up his pen and wrote the retort which shook the old State from mountain to sea, and which enhanced the chances of [14] the white supremacy advocates who were then planning for an uprising in November. "*Punish sin because it is sin*," concluded the editor, "*and not because the one who commits it is black.*" The article was commented upon by the press throughout the State, and "the affrontery of the Negro" in assailing white women bitterly discussed. *The Record* advanced from five to twenty-five cents a copy, so anxious was every one to see what the Negro had said to call for such ado. Threatening letters began to come in to the editor's office. "Leave on pain of death." "Stop the publishing of that of paper." "Apologize for that slander," etc. But the editor refused to apologize, "Suspend or quit." A meeting of citizens was called, and a colored man sent to advise the editor to retract, but he was obdurate. Immediately after the departure of the colored advocate, the owner of the building came in and told the editor that he was compelled to ask him to move out. He looked around the office so full of pleasant recollections. The face of "Little Shunshine," once the writer of the social column whose rolicksome disposition had robbed labor of its irksomeness in the work-room, beamed upon him from far over the seas, and rendered the quitting of the old home a much harder thing to do. But go he must. Colored friends hearing of his predicament rallied to his aid, and offered him at least a temporary asylum in one of their buildings. So the office of *The Record* was moved into Seventh Street. Excitement soon abated however, and *The Record* resumed its work. Those who are inclined to blame the editor of *The Wilmington Record* for the massacre of 1898 must remember that the article was written in August, and the massacre occurred in November; and that the editor of that paper did not leave Wilmington until a few days before the massacre, upon the urgent advice of friends. The whites of Wilmington had need to be afraid of the Negroes, and did not attempt to do violence until sufficiently reinforced from the outside, and the black citizens had been cut off from all means of defense. Editor Manley's reply to the Georgia woman was not the cause of the upheaval, but it was an excellent prbook when the election came on.
[15]

CHAPTER II.

The Colonel.

There strode out of a humble but neatly furnished dwelling in the Southern section of the city of Wilmington on a sultry morning in August, 1898, a man not over the average height, neatly dressed in a well-brushed suit of black. His full and well kept beard of mixed gray hung low upon his immaculate shirt front. His head classic and perfectly fashioned, set well poised upon shoulders as perfectly proportioned as an Apollo. His gray hair parted upon the side of his head, was carefully brushed over his forehead to hide its baldness, and from beneath abundant shaggy eyebrows, looked forth a pair of cold gray eyes. Though past sixty, he was erect, and his step was as firm as a man of thirty. This was "The Colonel," typical Southern gentleman of the old school, a descendant of the genuine aristocracy, the embodiment of arrogance.

The Southerners' definition of the term "gentleman" is a peculiar one. The gentleman is born, and there is no possible way for him to lose the title. He is a gentleman, drunk or sober, honest or dishonest, in prison or out of prison. He is a gentleman with the stains of murder unwashed from his hands. It is birth and not character with the Southerner, appearance, rather than worth.

While in New England settled the tanner, the wheelwright, the blacksmith, the hardy son of the soil who came over to escape religious persecution, and to serve God according to the dictates of his own conscience, with none to molest or make him afraid, in the South there settled England and Europe's aristocrat, lazy and self-indulgent, satisfied to live upon the unrequited toil of others.

The "Colonel," aside from having a brilliant war record, had also a lofty political career in North Carolina during and following the [16] reconstruction period. Twenty years or more ago he, in the height of his career, was the idol of Eastern North Carolina. "The silver-tongued orator of the East," his appearance in any town or hamlet was greeted with the greatest enthusiasm. Holidays were proclaimed and houses were decked with flags and bunting in honor of the hero of the day and hour. The workman forgot his toil, the merchant his business; old and young, little and big thronged the streets, women raised their little ones in their arms and cried, "See, the Colonel comes!" We listened with rapt attention to his superior eloquence, and no man was more deeply rooted in the affections of his people. We esteemed him too high to be low, too lofty in thought and aspiration to do a mean thing. Republican aspirants to Congress in those days were easily turned down by the Colonel who represented that district for three or more terms at the National Capitol. But there came a time when the Colonel's influence began to wane; whisperings were current that he was indulging too freely in the Southern gentleman's besetting sin—poker and mint julips, and that the business of the people whose interests he had been sent to look after was being neglected. Still Wilmingtonians' confidence in the Colonel did not slacken, and when the time for Congressional nominations came, we went to Fayetteville with bands playing and banners flying, and we cheered ourselves hoarse in order to quicken slumbering interest in the Colonel, but failed. Cumberland, Bladen, Mecklinburg and other counties came down unanimously in favor of one Shackleford, of the upper section, a name almost unknown to us, and New Hanover, which stood alone for the Colonel, was defeated. After the expiration of his term in Congress the Colonel went to his home in Wilmington, and resumed the practice of law. The last time that I visited the old city, the Colonel was solicitor in the Criminal Court. He had also moved out of his palatial dwelling on Third street, and sought cheaper quarters. Twenty years ago he would have scorned the thought of doing this deed which he was now contemplating as he strode down the street on this sultry August morning.

"I will carry this election or choke the river with their carcasses," he said slowly to himself. But why this ghastly sentence from the [17] mouth of a representative Wilmingtonian? What had plunged the Colonel into such a desperate state of mind? Poverty! lost honor, unsatisfied ambition. The Negro and the "low white" are prospering, holding positions in the city government that rightfully belong to first families who are better qualified to hold said positions and more entitled to the remunerations; but the changing of this order of things cannot be brought about by honest methods, so like the hungry wolf, the Colonel is preparing to make a desperate charge to carry the election and place himself in office, even if the streets of the old city flow with blood. Yea, although the usual state election time is some distance off, plans have been already secretly perfected not only to carry the election by the Democrats, but to reduce the Negro majorities by banishment, intimidation and murder.

Senator——, by invitation, had visited the state, and advised the carrying of the election with the shotgun, and had offered the loan of five hundred guns from South Carolina. Merchants, most of them in Wilmington, had promised to discharge all colored help who showed a disposition to vote, and had also subscribed to a fund for the purpose of purchasing powder, guns and dynamite. A railroad company operating into the city had subscribed five hundred guns. Stump orators had secured the aid of the poor whites both in the city and rural districts by promising them that by assisting to kill and chase the Negro from the city, the property owned by the colored citizens would be turned over to them. This was the work of hungry politicians who, to get office told an infamous lie, and were ready to deluge a city in blood just to get into office. Certain Negroes and white men had been listed for slaughter and banishment. Negro men and women who had had any difficulty in which they had gotten the best of a white person before the courts or otherwise, for even ten years back, were to be killed or driven from the city. Those who owned houses in white neighborhoods were to be driven out and their property taken. All this was being done quietly while the old city rested peacefully upon this smouldering volcano. The Negro, unaware of the doom that awaited him, went quietly about his work; but there were a few white men in the city who, although Southerners by birth and edu [18] cation, did not coincide with the methods adopted for the securing of white supremacy. Among these was Mr.

Gideon who could not be persuaded to assist in such a movement, even in the minutest way. A few mornings previous to the opening of my story, there had appeared in the columns of a small Negro journal edited in Wilmington, a short article which had been interpreted as an intent to slander white women. This had thrown the city into a fever of excitement, and dire threats had been made against the editor, and the flocking of the colored people to his aid had made the whites that much more bitter toward Negroes in general. But they soon quieted down, and waited the "final day." The Colonel feeling assured that this article in the Negro Journal would be the means of driving all lukewarm whites into line, leisurely strolled on this particular day toward the office of Mr. Gideon.

"Why, good morning, Colonel!" said Mr. Gideon, arising from his desk and extending his hand toward the Colonel who strode noiselessly across the large office and gently tapped him upon the shoulder. The Colonel sank into a chair, and opening the little sheet which he had drawn from his coat pocket, laid it on the desk before Mr. Gideon.

"Now, is it not time for white men to act?"

Mr. Gideon made no answer, but fastened his eyes upon the paper before him. The Colonel continued, "We have taken care of the Negro, paid his taxes, educated his children, tried to show to him that we were more interested in his well-being than the Yankee Radical Carpet-bagger he has chosen to follow; but he has persistently disregarded us, unheeded our advice, rode rough shod over us, and fretted us until patience is no longer a virtue. The Negro has reached the end of his rope. Emboldened by successful domination, and the long suffering of the white people of this community, this nigger has made an unpardonable attack upon our white women. Now, Gideon, if this article is not sufficient to stimulate you to join in with your brethren in driving the ungrateful nigger out of Wilmington and inducing white labor into it, you are not true to your race."

Mr. Gideon turned in his chair and faced the Colonel, "I have [19] previously read the article," he answered slowly "I have read also with—I must say—considerable disgust, the letters on the Negro question from the pen of Mrs. Fells, of Georgia, and the editorials of Kingston upon the subject; and to tell you the truth, Colonel, I must commend the boy for his courage; he was simply defending his race against the attack."

The Colonel jumped to his feet; "In the name of God, Gideon, do you believe that a nigger should answer a white man back?"

"Under certain circumstances, Colonel, I do. Mrs. Fells style is extremely brazen, and can we expect to harp with impunity upon the shortcomings of the Negro? Let us blame the right persons; those whose uncalled for assaults provoked the issuing of the article. But that's a small matter just at this time. I have refrained from entering into the scheme of driving out Negroes, because I am concerned about the business interests of this city; sit down, Colonel, sit down and hear me out. Now, when we have driven out the Negro, whose to take his place? We have tried the poor white."

"Why, encourage thrifty emigrants from the North." "Thrifty emigrants from the North," echoed Mr. Gideon.

"Invite labor unions, strikes, incendiarism, anarchy into our midst. Look at Illinois; can the South cope with such? The Negro we understand; he has stood by us in all of our ups and downs, stood manfully by our wives and children while we fought for his enslavement. After the war we found no more faithful ally than the Negro has been; he has helped us to build waste places and to bring order out of chaos. Now pray tell me where do we get the right to drive him from his home where he has as much right to dwell as we have?"

"Then you believe in Negro rule?"

"No!"

"Yes you do Gideon, or you'd not talk in that manner," replied the Colonel, now beside himself with rage. "Now, by heaven, we are going to put the Negro in his place. Look at our city government in the hands of ignorant niggers and carpet baggers. God did not intend that his white faced children were ever to be ruled by black demons," and the Colonel rose again and began to pace the floor.

[20] "Calm yourself, Colonel, calm yourself," said Mr. Gideon. "Now we ought to be ashamed of ourselves to raise the cry of Negro rule in North Carolina, when we so largely outnumber them. I admit that there are objectionable Negroes in Wilmington, Negroes who would greatly benefit the community by leaving it; but shall we slay the righteous with the wicked? Must the innocent and guilty suffer alike? Ten righteous men would have saved the cities of the plains."

"But they could nt be found," interrupted the Colonel.

"I warrant you they can be found here," calmly replied Mr. Gideon.

"We the white people of this community, have often given expression of our love and even veneration for such characters as Alfred Howe, Henry Taylor, John Norwood, George Ganse, John H. Howe, Thomas Revera, Joe Sampson, Henry Sampson, Isham Quick, and scores of others whom we must, if we do the right thing, acknowledge as the black fathers of this city. Thrifty and industrious Negroes have always been the objects of the envy of poor whites who will eagerly grasp the opportunity when given, to destroy the property of these people. While it is your object, Colonel, to carry the election, and triumph politically, they will murder and plunder, and when once licensed and started, you cannot check them. I see that they are being armed—a dangerous proceeding. Take care Colonel; I beg you to beware lest those guns in the hands of these people be turned upon you, and the best white people of this community be compelled to quit it. I listened with fear and apprehension a few evenings ago, to Fisher's harrangue to the poor whites of Dry Pond. They will take him at his word, for they are just that ignorant. Shall we for the sake of political ascension plunge Wilmington into an abyss of shame?"

"Now, Gideon," said the Colonel, "your talk is all nonsense, we are trying to extricate Wilmington from the slough of infamy into which it has been plunged by Radicals. We are going to elevate the white man to his place and regulate Sambo to his sphere, if the streets have to flow with blood to accomplish that end. Good niggers who know their places will be protected; but these half educated black rascals who think themselves as good as white men, must go. [21] 'Nigger root doctors' are crowding white physicians out of business; 'nigger' lawyers are sassing white men in our courts; 'nigger' children are hustling white angels off our sidewalks. Gideon, in the name of God, what next? what next?" and the Colonel bounded into the air like an Indian in a war dance. "White supremacy must be restored, and you Gideon will regret the day you refused to assist your white brethren to throw off the yoke of oppression. Good day, Gideon, good day"; and the Colonel stalked out of the office.

Uncle Ephraim, one of the old Nimrods who supplied Wilmington's markets with savory ducks and rice birds, stood with his gun on the corner of Front and Market streets that morning, as the Colonel briskly strode past on his way from the office of Mr. Gideon to the Court House.

"Good mawnin Co'nel," said Uncle Ephraim, saluting politely; but the Colonel did not as usual pause to crack a joke with the docile old darky; he did not even vouchsafe a nod of recognition, but moved hastily on his way. Uncle Ephraim stood and wistfully watched the Colonel until he turned the corner of Second and Market streets.

"Whoop! dar's er pow'ful big load on de Co'nel's mine sho. Dat white man didn' eben see me; an' I his ole bodysarbant, too." Uncle Ephraim strode slowly down Market street and entered the store of Sprague & Company. "Look yer!" said he, "I wants er bout fo' ounce powder an er few cap." The salesman shook his head.

"Wa fur yo' shake yer hed, you no got um?"

"We are selling nothing of the kind to darkies just now, uncle."

"But how I gwine fer kill duck?"

The salesman made him no answer.

Uncle Ephraim stood, looked about for a moment, then slowly sauntered into the street, and made his way to Joslins, in South Front street, but was also refused there. Going again to the corner of Market and Front Streets, he saw several white men and boys enter Sprague & Company and came out armed with shot guns and other firearms, and walk briskly away. "De ole boy is gwine to tun heself loose in dis yer town soon; fer I see um in de bery eye ob [22] dese bocra. I can't buy um, but see how de bocra go in an git um. Niggah, hit's time ter look er bout," — and Uncle Ephraim slowly walked up Front Street towards Morrow's.

[23]

CHAPTER III.

The Meeting In The Wigwam.

Three months have passed since the events narrated in the preceeding chapters. Chill winds are heralding the approach of winter. Wilmington is three months nearer its doom. Political warriors are buckling on their armour for the final struggle on the 8th of November which must result in complete victory for white supremacy, or indefinate bondage to Negro Domination (?)

Far out on Dry Pond in an old meeting house known as the Wigwam, the White Supremacy League has gathered. The old hall is poorly lighted but it is easy for the observer to see the look of grim determination on the faces of all present. It is a representative gathering. There is the Jew, the German, Irishman, Bourbon Aristocrat and "poor bocra." The deacon, the minister of the gospel, the thug and murderer. No one looking upon this strangely assorted gathering in a Southern community would for a moment question its significance. Only when politics and the race question are being discussed is such a gathering possible in the South. There is a loud rap: the hum of voices ceases. The individual who gives the signal stands at a small table at the end of the long narrow hall. One hand rests upon the table, with the other he nervously toys with a gavel. He is a tall, lean, lank, ungainly chap, whose cheek bones as prominent as an Indian's seem to be on the eve of pushing through his sallow skin. A pair of restless black eyes, set far apart, are apparently at times hidden by the scowls that occasionally wrinkle his forehead. His gray hair hangs in thick mats about his shoulders.

Teck Pervis had served in the war of secession under General Whiting, and was one of the many demoralized stragglers, who swept [24] before the advancing tide of the Union troops scampered through the swamps and marshes after the fall of Fort Fisher, to find refuge in Wilmington. During the Reconstruction period and many years following, he, with such characters as Sap Grant, Neal Simonds, Henry Sallins, Watson and others, made nights hideous on Dry Pond by their brawls and frolics. In introducing Teck Pervis to the reader, I wish to briefly call attention to that peculiar class in the South known as the "Poor Whites." Always an ignorant dependent, entirely different in every respect from the descendants of the Huguenots, Celt and Cavaliers that make up the South's best people; the origin of this being, who since the war has been such a prominent figure in the political uprisings and race troubles, and so on, is worthy of consideration. In the early centuries the English Government made of America what in later years Australia became—*a dumping ground for criminals*. Men and women of the Mother Country guilty of petty thefts and other misdemeanors were sent to America, bound out to a responsible person to be owned by said person until the expiration of sentence imposed, a stipulated sum of money being paid to the Crown for the services of the convict. At the expiration of their term of servitude these subjects were given limited citizenship, but were never allowed to be upon equality with those who once owned them. These indentured slaves and their descendants were always considered with contempt by the upper classes. The advance of American civilization, the tide of progress has arisen and swept over this indolent creature who remains the same stupid, lazy, ignoramus.

In Connecticut, New York, New Jersey, Delaware, Maryland, Virginia, North and South Carolina, and throughout the entire South are legion of this people, some of whom could not be taught the rudiments of arithmetic. When African slavery became established in America, white slavery was then tried in Australia where the treatment was so severe that thousands of them fled to the woods to become as wild in many instances as the natives. As the introduction of African slavery caused the indentured slave to depreciate in value as bond men, they were converted into overseers, patrolmen, Negro drivers to look for and to return runaway Negroes to their masters. [25] They were licensed to break up Negro frolics, whip the men, and ravish the women. But in the main the poor white subsisted by hunting and fishing. To him work was degrading, and only for "niggers" to do. A squatter upon the property of others, his sole belongings consisted of fishing tackle, guns, a house full of children, and a yard full of dogs. In Virginia, North and South Carolina he is known as "Poor Bocra," "Poor Tackie." In Georgia and Florida it's "Cracker," and there are few readers of current literature who are not familiar with that class of whites known as Clay Eaters of Alabama and Mississippi. Looked down upon by the upper classes, the poor white before the war was simply a tool for designing politicians. When war between the North and South became iminent, the poor white increased in value; for the aristocrat was adverse to being a common private. So they sought the poor white, appealed to his patriotism, pictured to him the wrongs heaped upon the South, and the righteousness of slavery. They drew glowing pictures of the Southern army's invasion of the North to thrash the Yankees, and pardon them in Faneuil Hall. The South freed, was to open her markets to the world. Her wealth was to be untold, while grass would grow on the sidewalks of Northern cities. Every poor white who shouldered a gun was to be elevated out of serfdom, be given forty acres of land, a "nigger" and a mule. Enthused by these glowing promises, the Southern poor white shouldered his gun and waded in: and no one reviewing the history of that immortal struggle would for a moment question the bravery of the Southern soldiers. They fought like demons. They invaded the North. They made the world wonder at Gettysburg.

Here Mississippi flushed with pride
Met Pennsylvania's deadly tide
And Georgia's rash and gallant ride
Was checked by New York's chivalry.
Here Alabama's rebel yell
Rang through the valleys down to hell
But Maine's decisive shot and shell
Cut short the dreadful revelry.

But the South's victorious armies did not reach Faneuil Hall. The air castles, the hopes of Southern prosperity and the poor whites [26] elevation and wealth were blasted, when two years after that gallant dash at Gettysburg, that ragged, starved, wretched host surrendered at Appomattox. The blasted hopes of the poor white caused him to drift further away from the aristocrat who had fooled him into a foolhardy and disastrous struggle. Land was cheap but he hadn't the money to buy it, and the aristocrat didn't have the "nigger" and the mule to give him. He grew lukewarm politically, got his rod and went a fishing. But with the Negro freed and enfranchised, and the Northern politician on the premises, the vote of the poor white became indispensible to the former Southern ruler who wished to hold his own politically. So a new battle cry was made, viz:—"Negro Domination," "Social Equality." But so lukewarm had the poor white become, that his song had to be sung with pertinacious fervor to make him do more than pause to listen.

"Do you want niggers to marry your daughters? Do you want niggers to sit in school beside your children? Do you want niggers on the juries trying white men? If you don't want such dreadful calamities to befall the South, go to the polls and do your duty!" "What'd he say? Niggers er marryin our darters? Niggers in skule wid we uns? Thet aint er goin ter du! Le' me see thet ticket!"

The Southern poor white has never had much of a hankering after "book larning." He's better than the "nigger" and that's all he cares to know. To be white means license to trample upon the rights of others. The cat's paw—the tool of the aristocrat, he stands ready always, to do the dirty work of lynching, burning and intimidation. Traveling South, especially on the East Coast, the train conductor only has to say to the colored passenger in a first class car but once that he must get out. If the passenger refuses, the conductor need not waste words; a telegram to Jessup or Way Cross, Ga., or Bartow Junction in Florida will call together a crowd of crackers, large enough to put the engine off the track if necessary. Like the dog in the manger, unable to pay for a first class ride himself, the poor white squats about railroad stations and waits for the opportunity to eject some prosperous Negro. I have known as many as two hundred to swarm around a train to put off one frail woman not over ninety pounds in weight.

This is the creature that is held up continually before the Negro [27] as his superior—an assertion that will ever be met with strong resistance. For while the Negro was a slave he is not a descendant of criminals.

"Gentermen," said Teck Pervis, "whils we air waitin fur ther kernul and other big uns ter errive, as cheerman uv the Dry Pond White Supreemacy Leeg, I wish ter keep this here meet'n warm by makin' er few broken remarks"— "Go ahead Teck, give us a speech" came from more than a dozen throats; "I wanter say jes here" he continued "thet ther white folks uv Wilmington, North Caliny hav tuk and stood nigger biggitty and hifullutin carryins on with moe patience then eny folks on top side er this green yerth" (Laughter and applause). "We po uns have jes layed er roun an slep till Mr. Nigger has trotted so fur er hed that I am feared we wont be able ter over take him." (Laughter). "They air in better houses then we po white uns, thur chilan air er wearin better cloes an er gittin moe larnin then our'n. An gentermen surs jes tackle eny er them little uns er'n an they'd surprise yer; why they kin spit latin faster then er terbacky worm kin spit terbacky. (Laughter). Who give ther nigger ther stick ter break our heads? *Who done it I say?* You rich white uns, thets who;" "But we'll do it no longer," said a voice from the audience. "We uns hepped yer ter fite yer battles," continued Teck, "an when thet war was ended, we did'n git ther nigger an mule yer promised, but we uns did'n kick powerful hard agin yer bekase yer did'n hev em ter giv us." (Laughter). "But you uns could er giv we uns ther wurk instid uv givin it ter good fur nuthin nigger bekase we po uns hev voted yer ticket rite er long an kep yer in office—

"I see ther kurnels on hand' so I giv way fur im," and Teck Pervis advanced to where the Colonel had paused to remove his overcoat. "Whats the matter with the Colonel? He's all right!" was uttered with a ring that shook the old wigwam. The Colonel, escorted by Teck Pervis, leisurely strutted to the centre of the hall. The Colonel had seen the time when he would have scorned the idea of being introduced to an audience by a low white. "Oh vain boast! who can control his fate?" He is now as poor as the poorest indentured slave, seeking to feed at the public crib by appealing to the passions and prejudices of the masses.

[28] "Gentlemen," says he, "it is needless for me to ask you to night whether or not you believe that the Anglo-Saxon race was ordained by God to rule the world. It is needless for me to say that the Anglo-Saxon proposes to carry out God's decree to the letter. (Applause). When God made man, he placed him over every other living creature to rule and govern, and that man was a white man. (Applause). When God said to man 'Have dominion over the beasts of the field,' He meant to include inferior races. These inferior races are to be kept in subjection by their superiors, and wherever and whenever they assume to dominate their superiors we are justified by our Creator in using every means available to put them down. The white people of North Carolina, the curled darlings of God's favor have by their long suffering gotten into such a state of subjection that it is time to act. (Applause). Wherever the Saxon has planted his foot, he has been a civilizer. He came to America, drove out the savage and made it the greatest nation on the face of the earth, (applause) and he has the right to govern it in its entirety from the humblest official to the executive head of the nation, (prolonged applause). We have for years been dominated by semi-civilized barbarians, flattered into the belief that they are as good as white people by unprincipalled Yankee carpet-baggers who have profited by their ignorance. Emboldened by the leniency of their superiors, Negroes have become unbearable. The government is corrupt, and so bold has the Negro become that the virtue of our women has been assailed by that black rascal, the editor of *The Record*—(cries of Kill him! Burn the scoundrel!) The snake is not to be scorched this time: we are going to make a clean sweep, and permanently restore white man's government. Our friends in other sections of the State, and even in adjoining States are in sympathy with us, and are willing to come in and help us," etc.

But why weary the reader with the Colonel's firey harangue? Although there is no foundation for such incendiary language the reader will soon see just how much misery it wrought upon a defenseless people. Fanned into fury by the rehearsing of imaginary wrongs by gifted tongues, the mob when once started astonished its leaders, who quailed and looked aghast at the hellish work they had inaugurated.
[29]

CHAPTER IV.

Mrs. Amanda Pervis.

"Whew! dis here win is er blowin pow'ful col fer Octoby. Ther ol sow was er tot'n straw yistedy and that means winter aint fur off. Shoo there! I never seed ther beat er thet ol hen; make hase ter gulp her own co'n down ter driv ther turkeys way from their'n." Thus spoke Mrs. Amanda Pervis as she stood in the door of her humble wooden dwelling on Kidder's Hill a brisk morning in October. "Thanksgiving haint fur off, an turkey meat's er gittin high. Shoo ther yer hussy!" "Who air yu er talkin ter Mandy?" said her husband coming to the door and peeping over his wife's shoulder. "I tho't er trader er some sort wus er passin." The wife turned and looked astonished at her husband. "Why fer ther lan sake, what's er comin over ye Teck Pervis? I tho't yer'd be fas er sleep after bein so late ter meetin las nite. I tho't yer'd tak yer res bein yer haint er goin er fishin!" "I felt kinder resliss like, and I tho't I jes es well be er gittin up," answered Teck, plunging his face into the basin of cool spring water that his wife had placed on the shelf beside the door. "Well hit won't tak me long ter git breakfus reddy," and Mrs. Pervis darted into the kitchen. Teck Pervis dipped his hands into the basin, poured the cool water on his head until his gray hair hung in thick mats over his face then leisurely drawing the towel from the nail beside the door, lazily wiped his head and face. The smell of fried bacon and delicious coffee arose from the kitchen; the rattling of dishes was to him sufficient token of the putting of victuals on the table. Teck Pervis sauntered in, sat down folded his arms upon the table, and sheepishly watched his wife as she flitted from place to place in the humble little kitchen. Mrs. Pervis paused, and her eyes met her husband's gaze. "Well what in ther wor'l is ter [30] matter Teck Pervis? Why air ye gazin at me so dis mornin, turn yer cup and tak yer coffy." "We uns had er interestin meetin las night," he said meekly. "Well mus yer put on er graveyard face ter day bekase yer had er interestin meetin las night? Don't put so much gravy on yer rice, hits ergin yer helth. Maria Tappin tol me yestidy thet her brother Tom was to be nitiated las night with er good meny other uns, an I 'lowed I'd here erbout hit, as my husban was er goin. Now yer air talkin erbout er interestin meetin the candidates muster all bin on han. " Teck Pervis looked pleadingly at his wife. Mrs. Pervis went on: "I am glad yer went ter loge meetin; er lot er them Red Shirt Varmints cum er roun las night er lookin fer yer to go with em ter that wigwam, and I was proud ter tell em that my husban' was not in politicks when it cum to killin colud folks ter git inter office, an that truth hit em so hard dey sneaked." Teck shuddered. During a series of revivals in the Free Will Baptist Church during the summer Teck Pervis had professed religion. A fierce struggle was going on 'neath his rugged breast. Must he tell the truth. The best whites were there even ministers of the gospel; but then preachers are not always on the right side; and Teck Pervis had promised his wife that he'd not allow himself to be a tool for hungry broken down aristocrats who only wished to use the poor as cats' paws. He took a big swallow of coffee, drummed nervously with his fingers upon the table. "I jes es well tell yer ther plain truth, Mandy," he said finally, "I got wi ther boys las night and went ter ther Wigwam, an was made Cheerman ov ther meetin. They lowed thet hit wus ter be ther mos importent meetin in ther campaign, an hit wus time fer white men ter be er standin tergither." "Teck Pervis," exclaimed the wife, "Hev I bin er rastlin'in prayer an pleadin ter ther Lawd in vain? Didn't I beg yer not ter fergit yer religion in jine-in wid sinners in doin eval?" "There aint er goin ter be eny killin done, Mandy, we air jes er goin ter skeer ther Niggers way from ther polls, an keep um frum votin. " "I know all erbout hit," broke in Mrs. Pervis. "Hit will en' in murder, for yer know thet Niggers won't be drove." "Why all ther big guns war there Mandy; merchints, lawyers, docters an ev'n preachers." "Laws e massy me!" exclaimed Mrs. Pervis. "An if ther shepod wus ther, yer kaint blame ther flock." "Teck Pervis [31] did I understan yo ter say that—" "Don't git excited, Mandy, yer jes es well git use ter ther new tern things air takin. Them preachers war thar bekase they sed hits time fur white uns ter stan tergither. Radicul rule mus be put down." Mrs. Pervis crossed her hands upon the table and looked resigned. "Teck, do tell me what preachers war they?" "Why ef yo own minister wus'n thar hiself I hope er hoppergrass may chaw me." "Teck Pervis, do ye mean ter tell me thet Brother Jonas Melvin wus at thet meetin?" "Yes, and Hoosay too, thet Presberteen man thet sines his name with er dubble D hung on ter ther een." "Jonas Melvin is er windin up his kerrare in Free Will Church. We'll hev no sich men fumblin wi ther werd ev God in our pulpit. I never did think them Presbyteens hed eny religion no way. They air full of book larnin, but havn't bin tech wit ther sparit. This Hussy is lik ther res er these hi tone preachers thet hang on ter this docterin thet ther yerth moves insted uv ther sun." "Hoosay Mandy. Why don't yer tak proper! Hoosay!" "Well, he jes oughter be named Hussy, fur he is er hussy. When ole sat'n meets them two at the cross-road thars er goin ter be er tussle now I tell yer." "Well now yer know thet ther scripter says cussed be Canyon, least wise thets the way Brother Melvin splained hit tother night, cussed be Canyon means cussed be Niggers." "Now Teck Pervis, wher is yer proof thet the scripter ment Nigger? I aint rusty un ther scripter ef I am er gittin ole." "Now, Mandy, yer know ther scripter reads thet Canyon was the son er Ham an wus cussed bekase his daddy laffed at ole Noey, bekase when he layed down ter sleep he didn't pull the kivver on his self proper like. When de ole man woke up the tother boys tole him what Ham hed done, he cussed Canyon Ham's son, and sed sarvant of sarvants shill he be. Ham wus ther Nigger boy in ther family, and we uns air carin out ther edicts of ther scripter when we try ter keep the Nigger cussed. Sarvant ov sarvants shill he be, an we air—" "Hol on, Teck Pervis," exclaimed his wife. "Let me git in er word kinder catiwompus like et leas. Now we air all ther time er lookin fer scripter ter back us up in our devalmint. Ther scripter don't say thet God'l mighty cussed Canyon, it says thet Noey cussed him, an ef Noey hed kep sober an b'haved hisself he wouldenter hed ter cuss at eny body. Whose teachin air we er follerin? Ole Noey's er our Blessed Lawd [32] an Saviour? He sed all things what soiver ye wood thet men should do ter yo, do ye evan so ter thim. Have yer back slided an fergot yer religin erready Teck Pervis?" Teck was dumb. "Yo Red Shirts Ruff Riders an broke down risterats kin go on an do yer devilment but mark what Mandy Pervis says, God'l Mighty will giv yu uns ther wurk er yer hans." "Why, Mandy, yo ought ter git er license ter preach, why you kin spit scripter lik er bon evangilis," and Teck Pervis reached over and slapped his wife upon the shoulder. This compliment from her husband stimulated the old lady to more earnest effort. "Now look er here," she continued. "What do them risticrats kere er bout the likes er we? In slave times we war not as good as their Niggers an ef we didn't get out ther way on the road, they'd ride their fine critters plum over us. They hed no use fer we uns unless hit wus ter use us fer somethin. Whan ther war broke out, of course they wanted der po'uns ter do ther fightin, an they kill me ole daddy bekase he would'n jine em. He didn't think it right ter tak up an fight agin the Union; an I can't fergit thet you'ns who did go ter ther fight ware promis'd er Nigger an er mule. But did yer git em?" Teck Pervis winced. Mrs. Pervis continued. "Now sich es ole Wade an Moss Teele an uthers air hungry ter git er bite at ther public grip, so they throw out bait fer yo uns ter nibble; an yer air fools ernuff ter nibble. Jane Snow tells me thet all ther big bug Niggers er goin ter be driv out, and we uns will git ther property and wash up in ther churches." "Thet wus promused," broke in Teck. "But who hes ther rite ter tek them critters property an giv hit ter yo uns?" replied Mrs. Pervis. "Teck Pervis yo may mark my words, but jes es soon es them broken down risticrats git er hol of ther gov'mint, jes es soon es yo po fools

help them, then yer kin go." Teck Pervis glared at his wife like a fierce beast at bay. He was Teck Pervis of old, the defiant, blood-thirsty rebel in the rifle pit glaring over the breastworks at the enemy. "Wese got ther guns!" he thundered, bringing his fist down upon the table, "an ef they dont give ther po' uns er show when ther city is took, why! we'd jes es leave kill er ristercrat as er Nigger, and we uns will do it. Wat yo say is right frum start to finish. We uns air watchin um; wese got ther guns, an we uns'll hold em till we see how things air goin ter wurk. Reach up there an han me my pipe Mandy."
[33]

CHAPTER V.

Molly Pierrepont.

"Sweet and low, sweet and low
Wind of the Western sea
Low, low, breathe and blow
Wind of the Western sea
Over the rolling waters go,
Come from the dying moon and blow
Blow him again to me
While my little one, while my pretty one sleeps."

This sweet old lullaby of Longfellow's, sung by a rich soprano voice floated upon the cool October air out from a beautiful and richly furnished suburban cottage in Wilmington. The singer sat alone at the piano. Though vulgarly called a "Negress," her skin was almost as fair as a Saxon's; and because of the mingling of Negro blood—more beautiful in color. She was gowned in an evening dress of gossamer material, ashes of rose in color. Her hair let out to its full length hung in silky profusion down her back. There were plain old fashioned half moon rings in her ears, and bands of gold upon her bare arms enhanced their beauty. No one will deny that among the women of mixed blood in the South, there are types of surpassing beauty. The inter-mixture of Negro and Saxon, Negro and Spanish and Indian blood gives the skin a more beautiful color than exists in the unadulterated of either race. While the mulatto and octoroon may reveal the Saxon in the fairness of the skin, the Negro reinforcement shows itself generally in the slight inclination of the lips toward thickness, the lustrous black of the eye and hair which is generally abundant and slightly woolly in texture. This is brought out plainly in the case of the Jew. Although centuries have passed since the Jews very extensively amalgamated with the dark races of Egypt and Canaan, [34] their dark complexions, lustrous black eyes, abundant woolly hair plainly reveal their Hamatic lineage. To pass through the Bowery or lower Broadway in the great metropolis at an hour when the shop and factory girl is hurrying to or from her work, one is struck by the beauty of Jewish womanhood. King David's successful campaigns placed Solomon over large dominions of Moabitish and Canaanitish peoples; and for the stability of his kingdom, Solomon took wives out of all of these nationalities; and Solomon's most favored wife was his black princess, Naamah, the mother of Rehoboam, his successor. The poet describes Naamah as the "Rose of Sharon, the most excellent of her country." The marriage of Solomon to his black princess was the most notable of any of his marriages; for that wonderful poem, "Solomon's Songs," is mainly a eulogy to this one of his many wives. "I am black but comely, O ye daughters of Jerusalem as the tents of Kedar, as the curtains of Solomon. Look not upon me because I am black, because the sun hath looked upon me." In the most beautiful language in the gift of the poets of that day Solomon converses with Naamah in the following dialogue: "Return, return O Shulamite; return, return that we may look upon thee." Naamah, "What will you see in Shulamite?" Solomon, "As it were a company of two armies."

We have conclusive evidence that the Southern gentleman did, and does sing such love ditties, and talk sweet nothings to the Southern black woman, and the woman of mixed blood, but unlike Solomon, he is too much of a coward to publicly extol her. During the slave period in the West Indian Islands a child born to a slave woman shared the fortunes of its father; and if the father was free, so was the child. But the American slave holder reversed that law so that he could humble the bond-woman and damn her offspring with impunity. Upheld by the law the Southerner sold his own daughter and sister into a life of shame. The pretty Negress and the woman of mixed blood brought extortionate prices in Southern markets. Northern sympathizers may talk of the New South, and the Southern orator may harp upon the shortcomings of the "inferior race," but on this line of thought and conduct, the Southern whites have not changed one whit. Before the war, Sambo only had a quitclaim on his black or mulatto [35] wife, and now the laws are so framed that he cannot defend the woman of his race against the encroachments of his white brother, who looks at the destruction of the Negro woman as only an indiscretion. The humble black fool is often forced away from his own wife or sweet-heart at the point of a revolver, cowed by the feeling that a manly stand against a white man might cause incalculable loss of life. Yet the advocate of Lynch Law pictures this humble fellow, this man who is afraid to attempt to defend his own home, as a reckless dare-devil, keeping the whites in constant terror. How incompatible these two traits of character. No; it is not the reckless dare deviltry of the Negro that terrorizes the South, but the conscience of the white man whose wrong treatment of a defenseless people fills him with fear and intensifies his hatred. He is determined to fill to overflow his cup of iniquity. Like Macbeth, he has waded in so far, that to return were as tedious as to go over. It matters not how loud the Southerner shouts about "the good-for-nothing Nigger," he still has the same old ante-bellum liking for the women of that race. Bishop Turner is the only honest and earnest advocate of Negro Emigration, the others have only a half-hearted leaning in that direction. If it were possible for emigration to become a reality, the Southern whites would be the hardest kickers against the scheme. The only beneficiaries from this wonderful enterprise would be the steamship companies; for after the hundreds of years of transportation are over, then excursion parties would be the order of the day for time immemorial. Our Southern gentleman will not be deprived of the Negro woman. There is no ocean too wide for him to cross; no wall too high for him to scale; he'd risk the fires of hell to be in her company, intensely as he pretends to hate her. Wilmington, North Carolina, the scene of that much regretted phenomenon—the fatal clashing of races in November, 1898, was not, and is not without its harems, its unholy minglings of Shem with Ham; where the soft-fingered aristocrat embraces the lowest dusky sirene in Paddy's Hollow, and thinks nothing of it. Molly Pierrepont whom I introduce to the reader in this chapter, is a type of Negro women whose progress along ennobling avenues is more hotly contested than any other woman in the South, because of her beauty. To decide between the honor with poverty offered by the [36] black man and the life of ease with shame offered by the white one is her "Gethsemine." Yet where love of honor has conquered, she has made a devoted wife and a loving mother.

Such a character as Molly Pierrepont was an exclusive luxury for gentlemen. The poor white could not afford to support a mistress who of course went to the highest bidder. Ben Hartright left the Wigwam before the close of the meeting in which he was so deeply interested, and proceeded directly to Molly's cottage; but he did not notice as he tipped lightly through the gate a cloaked and veiled form crouching down in the bushes a few yards away. He heard not the light footsteps as it drew nearer to be sure that there was no mistaking the visitor. Ben Hartright entered boldly; knocking was unnecessary, he was master there. The furniture and hangings were all his purchase, even the expensive jewels that the woman wore. The figure on the outside drew still closer, peered in, tip-toed upon the piazza, pressed the ear against the window to catch as much as possible of what went on within. Only a few minutes did it tarry however. As the door swung open, Molly arose from the piano and advanced with outstretched arms to meet him.

"Hello, Ben! I thought you were to be here by eight to-night."

Ben Hartright sank upon a sofa and gently drew the girl down beside him before he assayed to answer her.

"Well, Molly, you must remember that I am in politics now," he said, kissing her fondly, "and I must attend the different meetings, business before pleasure you know. We are in the most exciting period of the campaign; a campaign the like of which has never before been experienced in North Carolina. We are organized and determined to save the State to the Democratic party and make white supremacy an established fact if we have to kill every Nigger and Nigger-hearted white man in it. To make assurance doubly sure, we are arming ourselves, and seeing to it that no Nigger shall buy an ounce of powder, and every Nigger man and woman is to be searched and what weapons they have taken away that no white man's life may be endangered. There are some Niggers and white men who must be killed, and they are carefully listed."

Ben Hartright unbosomed to Molly the plots of the White Su [37] premacy League in all its blood-curdling details, naming every man and woman who were to be the victims of the mob's fury.

"Do you think that a very brave thing to do?" asked Molly at the conclusion of Ben's recital.

"Oh, anything is fair in dealing with Niggers," answered Ben. But the look of astonishment in Molly's black eyes suddenly brought Ben Hartright to the full realization that he was revealing the secrets of his klan to one of the race he was plotting to massacre.

"Of course we don't include such as you, Molly," he said, lightly tapping her on the shoulder. "You are no Nigger, you are nearly as white as I am."

"Nearly as white," echoed Molly with a sneer. "Do you mean to try to choke it down my throat that my whiteness would save me should your people rise up against Niggers in Wilmington? Honestly, Ben Hartright, do you mean that?" Molly arose from the sofa and stood up before her lover that she might the better study his face. Hartright was silent.

In Southern legislative halls white minorities in old Reconstruction days ruled Republican majorities by appealing to the vanity of light-skinned Negro representatives.

"You are almost white, why vote with them Niggers?" Ben Hartright was using the old tactics; he had realized that he perhaps had been careless with his secrets. "What I really mean, Molly, is that you are a friend of white people—that is you are not one of those Nigger wenches who want to be er—er—ladies—that want Nigger dudes to raise their hats to them—want to be like white people you know."

"I understand," said Molly.

"We white gentlemen believe in having colored girl friends, and we always stand by them no matter what happens." Molly momentarily eyed the ceiling.

"Benny, did you ever read Uncle Tom's Cabin?"

"Yes, I have," answered Ben, but it has been too long ago to remember very much of its contents.

"Why? Everybody should read that book it seems to me; read and read again Cassie's story of her love for the man who after prom [38] ising to protect and defend her, sneaked away and sold her. Cassie was almost white. Cassie was a white man's friend, and to that man she was true; but Cassie's story of betrayal, disappointment, misery at the hands of that long haired brute who afterwards became her master, would make the strongest heart weep. *You will stand by your colored girl friend.* Perhaps you think you would, but I doubt it, Ben Hartright. When that time comes that the two races are arrayed against each other, my fair complexion will be of no avail. I am a Nigger, and will be dealt with as such, even by the man who now promises me protection."

Ben Hartright quailed under Molly's biting sarcasm. He was unprepared for this change of front on the part of his mistress. His pretention of love were not sufficient to create in Molly a feeling of security.

"Then d'm it all! you as good as tell a gentleman to his teeth that he lies then?" said he doggedly.

"No; I don't mean to say that you lie. What you say to me *now*, you may earnestly mean, but under circumstances just mentioned, you would deny that you ever knew me. What you have revealed tonight concerning your aims and plots, portrays to my mind just who and what you are, and just who and what I am. Samson has revealed his secret to his Delilah, and its Delilah's duty to warn her people of the dangers that await them. Men whose lives are threatened must be warned; women who are in danger of being ignominiously dealt with must be put upon their guard; must know that these defenders of virtue, these Southern gentlemen who are thirsting for the blood of a slanderer (?) of white women are hypocrites, who strain out a gnat and swallow a camel."

"By the thunder, what do you mean by such language?" and Ben Hartright arose from the sofa and glared at the girl, his eyes flashing. "Do you know that you are talking to a gentleman?"

"Be careful," said Molly, "You wouldn't have the women for whom you would be so chivalrous know who Ben Hartright *really is*, would you?"

"Why, what's the matter Molly?" said Hartright in a more subdued voice. "Have you joined the sanctified band?"

[39] "No; but I realize as never before just who and what I am, and your trying to flatter me into the belief that I am better than black women who try to be pure, is a revelation to me who and what *you are*. There are men whom you have named to be killed whose only offense is that they are respectable and independent; and women who are hated because they are not easy victims such as I am—women who will live honestly upon bread and water. These are colored people who have so much confidence in the better class of white people, that they would not believe that such a plot is being laid for their destruction."

Ben Hartright put his arms around Molly's waist. "I thought you were a true friend of white people, Molly; but I find that you are not, so let's drop the unpleasant subject. If the Niggers keep away from the polls, and don't attempt to run a ticket, there will be no trouble; but if they persist in defying the whites, there'll be hell. But all pretty Nigger gals such as you will be all right."

"Unhand me!" said Molly, twisting herself from his grasp. "Go tell your hypocritical associates in crime that the deed they are about to commit will recoil upon their own heads, and upon the heads of their children."

"But—er—now Molly—"

"Go!" hissed Molly, pointing to the door.

Ben Hartright walked slowly to the door paused and wistfully eyed Molly who stood with uplifted hand pointing in that direction. "Oh, you are quite full of race pride just now, but when it comes to deciding between the easy life that a white man pays for and Nigger drudgery, you'll doubtless change your tune. I leave you to reflect."

Hartright walked out. Molly sank upon the sofa and buried her face in her hands. "How true!" she sobbed. "What have I done?" but she rose and her anguish was gone in a twinkling. "Easy life! Drudgery! But *here I swear from this hour Molly Pierrepont will live no longer such a life*."

Ben Hartright reached his home in Orange street about three o'clock, noiselessly opened the door and strode up to his apartments, thinking he would get to bed without disturbing his young wife; but she was not there. The bed remained as it was when the chambermaid left [40] it that morning, after giving it its finishing touches. Ben Hartright looked about the room in wild amazement. He drew out his watch, scanned its face eagerly. "By ginger!" he exclaimed, "it's past three o'clock. Wonder where is Emily? This is indeed something unusual." Thinking perhaps that his child might have taken ill during the night and that his wife had remained in the nurse's room with it, he crossed the hall and rapped upon the door; a second rap brought the nurse to the door rubbing her eyes. "What's the matter, Fannie; is the baby sick?"

"No, sah!" answered the girl.

"Isn't Miss Emily in there?"

"No, sah; Mr. Benny she aint in heah, sah."

"*Where in the thunder is she then?*" roared Ben Hartright, now beside himself with rage. "*Is this the way you look after your mistress?*" and he seized the already frightened girl by the shoulders and shook her vigorously, turned away before she could utter a word of excuse, and bounded down to his mother's apartments.

Mrs. Hartright, aroused by the noise above, was just emerging from her door to learn the cause of it all. "Why, what's the matter, son?" she questioned gently, as Ben, both angry and frightened, strode up to where she stood.

"Didn't you hear me asking Fannie where Emily is? Didn't you know that she hasn't been in her room, and here it is nearly four o'clock in the morning!"

"Emily went out just after tea, and I thought she had returned," answered the mother. "Perhaps she went walking with some of her girl friends, was taken ill and had to stop at one of their homes. Wait Benny, I'll dress and help you to look for her."

Ben Hartright turned and walked slowly to the door and paused to wait for his mother. There was a turn of the door latch, a vigorous twist of a key in the lock; the door flew open and Emily Hartright walked in. She apparently did not see her husband who stood and eyed her angrily as she entered and began to ascend the steps to her room.

"Emily," said Ben, following and seizing his wife by the arm. "Are you mad, if not explain this extraordinary conduct of yours. [41] Where have you been?" She turned, gazed into her husband's eyes for a moment, then with one vigorous tug, she wrenched her arm from his grasp and proceeded up the steps. The mother by this time had joined her son, and they both followed the young lady who had entered her room and was removing her wraps.

"What's the matter my darling?" said

Mrs. Hartright, throwing her arms around her daughter's waist. "I was so troubled about you. What kept you out so late, Emily?"

"Wait, mother, until I have rested and composed myself, then I will explain," answered Emily, softly.

Ben had sank into a chair and sat with his chin resting upon the palm of his hand. Emily sat upon the side of the bed.

"Men go night after night," she said, "stay as long as they please, and return in whatever condition they please; and to queries of their wives, they are evasive in their answers; but when a woman takes the privilege of exercising her rights—"

"*Her rights*," roared Ben, jumping to his feet. "A lady goes out of her residence, leaves her servant and relatives in ignorance of her destination, returns at four o' clock in the morning to tell anxious husband and mother about *her rights*! We'll have a direct explanation from you, Mrs. Hartright, without preambling."

"I'll not be bullied, Ben Hartright," answered the young wife calmly. "Remember that when you married *me*, you didn't marry a chambermaid or housekeeper, but a lady of one of the first families of Virginia, and such people brook *no bullying*," and Emily arose and glared at her husband like a tigress.

Ben Hartright quailed. Never had he seen his little wife in such a state of anger and defiance.

"If you are man enough to reveal your whereabouts until the small hours of the morning, you can tell where your wife was."

Ben Hartright raised his eyes from the floor and looked at his wife in amazement.

"When you entered the house of your mistress, Molly Pierrepont, to-night, I saw you. I, your *wife*, whom *you* swore to honor and protect, saw you. She saw you embrace and kiss a Negro woman, the woman of a race whom you pretend to despise, and whom you and [42] your pals are secretly scheming to cold bloodedly murder and drive from their homes. Take care! God knows your hypocrisy and the deeds you commit will recoil upon your own heads."

"Emily, are you mad?" gasped the elder lady who stood as if transfixed to the floor.

"Ask him," returned the young lady, "he knows whether or not I utter the truth, or whether I am a victim of a beclouded brain. He knows that he has wronged me; he knows that he has lied to me. I care not for your frowns. *You* a gentleman? You hate Niggers, yet you can embrace one so fondly. I will no longer live with such a gentleman, who night after night under the excuse of 'clubs' and 'business' spends his time away from his wife, and in company of a Negro woman. I am going home to my people."

"Now, Emily," said the elder Mrs. Hartright, "don't start a scandal; remember that you are a Southerner. Southern people do not countenance the airing of unpleasant family matters!"

"Yes," replied the young lady, "this fear of airing family troubles on the part of our women, has made us slaves, while the men are licensed to indulge in all manner of indecencies with impunity. I will be the first Southern woman to sever the chain of 'formality,' and cry aloud to the world that I leave my husband because of his unfaithfulness. It is my right, and I will exercise that right."

Ben who had again sank into his seat arose and advanced toward his wife to sue for forgiveness.

"Don't touch me!" she cried, with uplifted hand. "The cup is full. Go back to her who has monopolized the best portion of your time since you have married me."

Ben Hartright sank again into his chair and buried his face into his hands.

"Now, my darlings, let mother be the daysman between you," said the elder Mrs. Hartright, coming near carressing the young wife. "Benny knows just to what extent he has wronged you my dear, and I believe him honest enough and manly enough to acknowledge it, and sue for forgiveness. I leave you to yourselves. God grant that you may be enabled to peacably settle your difficulties satisfactorily to you both, without giving license to Madame Gossip. God bless [43] you." Kissing Emily, Mrs. Hartright descended to her room.

Ben Hartright succeeded in patching up matters with his wife by promising to live a more honest life, only to break it, which caused her to make good her threat and leave him.
[44]

CHAPTER VI.

The Union Aid Society Holds a Meeting.

The home of Mrs. West was one of the many snug little cottages owned by the colored inhabitants of that section of Wilmington known as "Camp Land." It also had the distinction of facing Campbell Street, the main thoroughfare of that portion of the city. Although Mrs. West knew something of slavery as it existed in North Carolina, she was free born; her grandfather having purchased his freedom, and afterwards that of the rest of the family before her birth. The rule that the free Negro was a shiftless being more to be pitied than envied by slaves, was not without many exceptions in North Carolina. There were many Negroes in old North Carolina who by grasping every opportunity to earn an extra dollar by working for neighboring planters when their own tasks were done, and making such useful articles as their genius could contrive, often after years of patient toiling and saving would often astonish their masters by offering to purchase their freedom. There were others who paid to their masters annually a specified sum of money for their time, that they might enjoy the control of their own affairs as much as possible.

For many years before the war my father did public carting in the town of Fayetteville as a free-man, his master receiving a certain amount of his earnings. Of course there were free Negroes whose conception of freedom was a release from manual toil, and who like poor whites, lived a shiftless indolent life, following the sunshine in Winter and the shade in Summer.

[45] Free Negroes in North Carolina had the right to purchase property and

enjoy other limited privileges. The parents of Mrs. West, known as Burchers, emigrated to the West in the forties, where their children could be educated. After the war Mrs. West, with her husband whom she had met and married in Ohio, returned to North Carolina, prepared to enter upon the work of uplifting the newly emancipated of their unfortunate race; and now well advanced in years, she could look over many years of active useful service in the cause of her people. It was the evening for the regular monthly meeting of the Union Aid Society of which Mrs. West was President, and several members had already arrived; but in such a season such business for which a society of this kind was organized would doubtless be neglected, so pregnant was the air with the all absorbing subject—politics.

But the Union Aid Society is composed exclusively of women. What of that? Some of our most skilled politicians in the South are among the women of both races. Although they do not take the stump and sit upon platforms in public assemblages, they are superior house-to-house canvassers, and in their homes noiselessly urge the men to do their duty. For earnest persistence and true loyalty to the party of her choice, the Negro woman of the South outdoes her sister in white. Give the ballot to the women of the South, and give her dusky daughters an equal show, and a Solid South would be a thing of the past; for the Negro woman is the most loyal supporter of Republican principles in that section. So radical is the Negro woman, that it is worth a husband's, or brother's, or sweetheart's good standing in the home or society to assay to vote a Democratic ticket. Such a step on the part of a Negro man has in some instances broken up his home. The Spartan loyalty of the Southern white woman to the Confederacy and the Lost Cause was not more marked than is the fidelity of the Negro woman to that party which stood for universal freedom and the brotherhood of man, and whose triumphant legions so ignominiously crushed Freedom's sullen and vindictive foe. Although the Government provides for the annual placing of a small flag upon the grave of each of the thousands of heroes now sleeping in the Southland, it is the dusky fingers of the Negro woman, perfumed by [46] the sweet incense of love and gratitude that places the lilac, the rose and forget-me-not there.

The Northern white woman in the South, in order to maintain her social caste, generally allows her patriotism to cool. But the Negro woman sings patriotic airs on each 30th of May as she twines wreaths of pine to lay upon the graves of those *who died for her*. Of course, these women who had gathered in the parlor of Mrs. West's cottage were intensely interested in the coming election in Wilmington, and were ready to discuss the event with all the fervor of their patriotic souls. "Ladies," said Mrs. West after the prayers had been said, and the minutes of the previous meeting read, "I confess that for the first time since my election to the presidency of this society, I feel an inclination to waive the transaction of its regular business, so depressed am I over events now crowding upon us." "I believe thats the case with every one," answered Mrs. Cole. "I have received a letter from the Chairman of the Executive Committee," continued Mrs. West, "stating that so grave is the situation all over the State that he is advised by the Governor himself to withdraw Republican candidates from the field—a request without a precedent in North Carolina."

"It would never do to show such cowardice!" said Mrs. Cole. "If I were chairman of that committee I'd put the ticket in the field and go to the polls if the devils were around it as thick as shingles upon a housetop." "I was of the same mind" answered Mrs. West, "but when the Governor of the State—when brave Daniel Lane has become apprehensive, I can appreciate the gravity of the situation. I have seen that man walk undismayed through the streets of Wilmington during very turbulent periods in her history. I see that in the upper section of the State the Democrats have already organized Red Shirt Brigades who are riding through the rural districts terrorizing Negroes, and we may look for the same to take place in Wilmington. Silas writes that they are determined to carry the election. He has received two threatening letters and is afraid. You are aware that that monster has been, and is advising the whites in our State to copy South Carolina's method of carrying elections, and they are heeding his advice. I am compelled to acknowledge despite my [47] previous confidence in the integrity and honesty of our North Carolina white people that my faith is getting shaky. The buying of guns and other weapons by poor whites who are often unable to buy food, means something. It means that the rich are going to use them to perform the dirty work of intimidation and murder if necessary to carry this election." "Colored men must show their manhood, and fight for their rights," exclaimed Mrs. Wise the secretary who had laid down her pen and was attentively listening to the president's talk. "But how are they to do it?" asked Mrs. West; "My son tells me that there is not a store in the city that will sell a Negro an ounce of powder. The best thing to do—if such things should happen—is to stay in our homes, and advise the men to be cool. Rashness on their part would be all the excuse the unprincipalled whites would want to kill them. Editor Manly's reply to Mrs. Fell's letter in August is now brought forward to be used by their stump orators to fan the flames of race hatred." "I wish he hadn't written it," interrupted Mrs. Cole. "It was a truth unwisely said," answered Mrs. Wise, "and by a man who meant to defend his own; so let us make the best of it. I would not have Editor Manly feel for a moment that we are such ingrates as to say anything against him."

"The most important thing that I intended to mention, and which makes me feel that our situation is a critical one," continued Mrs. West, "was a letter that came this morning from Molly Pierrepont." "Molly Pierrepont!" echo every one almost in one breath. "Poor erring girl!" said Mrs. Wise slowly. "What has happened her?" "Molly has written me a long and even affectionate letter. She writes, '*Ben Hartright confided to me* the other night the ghastly plans of the Rough Riders, a band made up from the most respectable of the whites. They are to be reinforced from all over the State, and even from other States for the purpose of killing and driving from Wilmington objectionable blacks and whites, John Holloway, Nicholas McDuffy, Editor Manly, John Brown, Lawyers Scott, Moore and Henderson, George Z. French, Thomas Miller, Ariah Bryant, McLane Lofton, Pickens and Bell and others of prominence and independenence are to be special marks of vengeance. I beg you my dear Aunt Betty, warn these people. I shall take it upon myself to give the alarm, for these are my people.'

[48] "There is some good in this wayward child after all," said Mrs. West, pushing her spectacles back, and looking up. "But who of these people would believe that such was in store for them? These men would not leave their homes without a severe struggle." "The Government should protect its citizens in their rights," said Mrs. Wise. "Government? Bah!" answered Mrs. West. "Here's the highest official of the State afraid for his own life." "Well if the Governor is incapable of coping with the situation, the President has the power to send in the troops," said Mrs. Cole. "Yes, but will he use that power? I don't believe McKinley is going to do anything to offend the Southern whites if they kill every Negro in the South. The interests of an alien race are too trivial to risk the sundering of the ties that are supposed by the North to bind the two sections. Each State according to the Southern view, is a sovereignty itself, and can kill and murder its inhabitants with impunity. There is no John Brown, Beecher, nor Sumner, nor Douglass, Garrison, Phillips and others of that undaunted host who were willing and did risk persecution and death for us; this generation has not produced such precious characters. God is our only helper and we must look to Him for deliverance. We are living too well for the broken down aristocrats and poor whites who are disappointed because we are not all domestics.

"Molly expresses her intention to call, and I was hoping she would come before you all left. Perhaps you know Molly Pierrepont, for a woman of her reputation cannot help being known to a small community; but you are not all aware of the fact that I raised her, and took special pains to give her a good education, and I thought she'd requite me by trying to lead a useful life." "But you know Mrs. West, that Negro girls of attractiveness in the South have a great battle to fight, if they wish to be pure," said Mrs. Wise. "That's very true" answered Mrs. West; "I have often pondered over the thought since she left me five years ago, that the conditions under which she was born may have had something to do with shaping her course in life. We, innocent as we may be, must suffer for the iniquities of our parents. Before the war, there lived in Brunswick a large slave owner by name of Philpot. He was the father of [49] Molly's mother, one of his slaves. After the surrender, this woman did not leave the plantation of her master but remained there until her death. The child, Molly's mother, whose name was Eliza, at the time of her mother's death was a pretty lass of fourteen; so attractive that the father then an old man could not curb his brutal passion. It is needless for me to speak plainer ladies. There is a passage of Scripture which reads as follows: 'The dog has returned to his vomit, and the sow that was washed is wallowing in the mire.' The young mother brought the child to Wilmington, gave her to me, and disappeared. Molly was then about four years old. Those who knew of me and my affairs know how carefully I raised the girl. She graduated from Hampton with honors, has a fair musical education, and a voice that might have made her a fortune. Imagine how proud her foster mother was when she returned home from school, so full of promise. If she would only leave this place and seek to live a better life in some strange community I would be more content. It would be hard for her to do so here. This Ben Hartright and another white gentleman had a free fight over her about a month ago. Ben was prevented from using his pistol by the girl's timely interference. That fiend of Georgia who is urging the men of her race to revel in the blood of their fellows, would do them more good by urging upon them the necessity of good morals. Doubtless this Ben Hartright is one of the leaders of this proposed raid in Wilmington to drive out undesirable citizens, yet he is so low morally, that he leaves a richly furnished home, a refined wife and pretty child to fight over a Negro woman, for such he has I hear." "But this letter proves that there are redeemable qualities in Molly despite her birth and bad life." "Magdalene made a devoted follower of Christ, you know," said Mrs. Wise; "with God's help, she can if she wills, pull away from her present surroundings and be a good woman." "Yes, she says in her letter that *'never did the full realization of what I am, come so plainly before me, as when this villian so cooly told me of his plans. I drove him from my presence as I would a dog.'* This shows that Molly's race pride is not entirely blunted by dissipation and unholy living. I counsel you all ere you depart, to remember that we are at the mercy of the whites, and each one of us [50] should do all in our power to show our men the wisdom of coolness. By this, with God's help, we may be able to avert the evil threatened. I declare the Union Aid Society adjourned, subject to the call of the president." [51]

CHAPTER VII.

Molly's Atonement.

A few evenings after the unpleasant interview between Molly Pierrepont and Ben Hartright, Silas Wingate, chairman of the Republican Executive Committee, sat alone in his office. In that morning's mail had come to him a letter from the Governor, full of discouraging news as to the chances of Republican success throughout the State, and advising that for the safety of life Republican candidates be withdrawn from the field—a request unprecedented in the history of the State. "This would be too cowardly a backdown," he soliloquized. "The situation is not so serious perhaps as the

Governor imagines. Such bluffs the Democrats have resorted to more than once before, but they didn't deter us in the least. We put our ticket in the field and fought hard for its election." But never before had the chairman of the Executive Committee seen in New Hanover County such grim and warlike activity on the part of the Democrats. The arming of the poor whites, the hiring of sterner implements of war, secret house-to-house meetings, and the stern refusal of dealers to sell a black man a deadly weapon of any description or as much as an ounce of powder meant something more than bluff. Yet so strong was the faith of Mr. Wingate in the integrity of the better classes of Wilmington's white citizens that he was slow to grasp the situation although the evidence was so overwhelming. He took the letter from the desk and read it for the fourth time since receiving it, riveting his eyes long and intently upon the signature affixed. Of all the years he had known the Governor he had never known him to shrink or show cowardice in any form whatever, although he'd passed through such crises as would tend to test the mettle [52] of any man, it matters not how brave. "Surely the situation must be terrible!" finally observed Mr. Wingate, throwing the letter upon the desk and whirling around in his chair. "I will call a meeting and put the matter before the committee. When that man says back down then surely doomsday is not far off."

There was a timid knock at the door. Feeling that perhaps it was one of his colleagues dropping in for a chat upon the all-absorbing topic of the day, Mr. Wingate did not rise or turn his face in that direction, but simply bid the visitor enter. The latch was timidly turned, followed by light footsteps, accompanied by the rustle of skirts, and before he could turn his head to see who this unexpected visitor might be, the figure had glided up to his chair and two soft hands were pressed over his eyes. "Now, just guess who it is. I will not release my hold until you do," was the soft command. "Now, as I was expecting only politicians to-night and, of course, no visitor in petticoats, I should be excused from trying to guess who you are on these grounds," answered Mr. Wingate, trying to force the hands which were firmly pressing down upon his eyes. "In such times as these you are likely to see even the women in the forefront in the fray, and doing even more than merely making calls," returned the visitor, releasing her hold and stepping in front of Mr. Wingate. "Why, Molly Pierrepont! What brings you here?" exclaimed Mr. Wingate, rising and staring at his visitor, who unceremoniously sank into a chair. "I am somewhat interested in this campaign myself—astonishing intelligence I know," calmly replied the visitor; "yet I am going to astonish you more by saying that I have information to impart to the chairman of the Executive Committee that will be of great value to him in conducting this campaign. " Molly's calm demeanor, so unlike a woman of her disposition and temperament, struck Mr. Wingate somewhat humorously. Molly Pierrepont, having chosen a life of shame that she might—if only clandestinely—associate with and enjoy the favors of the men of the white race, would be the last person of the race to take a stand in its defense to give aid to the Negro in his combat with the white man, politically or otherwise. Women of Molly's stamp, possessing no [53] race pride, had never been race defenders, so it was plausible for Mr. Wingate to feel that the woman was jesting, or that she was sent by his enemies into his camp as a spy. "In our present dilemma the Republican Committee stands much in need of information and advice," said Mr. Wingate, slowly. "Things are assuming quite a serious aspect; you are in position to get a good deal of information as to the maneuvers of the enemy. But, my dear girl, if you are here to aid us, have you counted the cost?" Mr. Wingate knew that Molly Pierrepont was the mistress of one of Wilmington's best citizens, a bitter Democrat, and a reputed leader of the White Supremacy League; that she was well cared for, that her gowns, etc., equaled in quality and construction those of her paramour's wife, and, considering her love for such ease and luxury, to come out and reveal the doings, and openly denounce the schemes of the party of her paramour, was a sacrifice that a woman of her character was not generally ready to make—in fact, such thoughts did not find lodgment in her brain. In the flattering embrace of the Philistine all noble aspirations ordinarily become extinct. Mr. Wingate's interrogation was followed by a brief pause, which caused Molly to move uneasily in her chair. "I see, Silas Wingate, that you question my sincerity," she said, slowly. "I can't blame you, though. It is perfectly natural for such as I to be arrayed with the whites or be neutral, stifling all thoughts of being of service to my wronged people, because my life belies it. But I am sincere, Silas; believe me," and Molly reached over and laid her hand upon the arm of Mr. Wingate, whose look betrayed his incredulity. "In spite of the lowliness of my birth, and the life I have chosen, some good remains in me." She went on: "My fair complexion and life of ease have not made me forget that I am identified with the oppressed and despised." "Thank God! thank God!" said Mr. Wingate, his face brightening. "There is a ring of sincerity in your voice, my dear, that banishes doubt." "I come to-night to warn you, Silas," continued Molly. "Before many moons Wilmington will be the scene of a bloody race war. Ben Hartright is my medium of information. He came to my house last evening, and, imbued with the feeling that I was [54] in sympathy with the white element, revealed to me the dastardly plot in all its blood-curdling details." Mr. Wingate trembled and shook like an aspen leaf as Molly named the men and women singled out as victims. "These people have ample time now to make good their escape. Tell them, Silas, that the best whites are in this move, and they are determined to carry it to the bitter end, and their only safety is in flight. Ben tells me that the plans are well laid, that men will be here to assist in the dirty work from as far South as Texas. I listened patiently to Hartright's recital and then denounced him and his cohorts as infamous cowards!" "Did you dare?" exclaimed Mr. Wingate, gazing eagerly into Molly's face. "I drove him from my presence." Mr. Wingate drew nigh and laid his hand caressingly upon Molly's head. "You have risked much," he said, eagerly. "I fully realize that," returned Molly. "When he had left me, what I had said and done came home with its full force, but, like Jephthah, I had sworn, and will not go back; and here now, as I did then, I swear with uplifted hand to renounce forever my life of shame, and will be no longer a Magdalene!" "Angels record thy vow in heaven," said Mr. Wingate. "You can, with God's help, be true to your vow, for Magdalene, who became one of the faithful, was a greater sinner than you, Molly." "But Magdalene perhaps never threw away the opportunities for good that I have," answered Molly, who had arisen and begun to pace the floor. "Magdalene is not charged with having spurned the love and sent to a premature grave a man who offered to honor and protect her through life." "Don't brood over the past, Molly," said Mr. Wingate, a grass-covered mound in Pine Forest Cemetery rising before him. "Let the dead past be gone." "I will not! I cannot!" said Molly, pausing. "The past will spur me to higher aims in the future. I never can forget the time that Harold came to make a last plea to me to be his wife, expressing his willingness to make every sacrifice for my happiness. He had bright hopes of success in his profession. Yet I spurned his offer to live a life of shame with a white man. You know he went to Macon afterwards, and there as a physician built up quite a lucrative practice. He wrote me often; he spoke of his [55] prosperity and his unhappiness without me to share it. He could not forget me. I tried to forget him by plunging deeper into sin. It's some three years ago now since the last letter came, in which he said, 'I am dying! dying! dying for you!' I tried to make light of it as perhaps merely a jest. But, Silas, you know that it's quite two years now since they buried the heart which I had broken in Pine Forest Cemetery. Harold! Harold! If I could only call you back with those sunny days of innocence. No one knows but God what anguish I have suffered since you left me. But I was unworthy of you, Harold, unworthy!" The woman had bowed her head upon the desk and was sobbing convulsively. "Oh, that you could come back to me, Harold! Harold, tender and true. How gladly would I accept your offer now, Harold. You would forgive me, unworthy me." Her voice sank into an incoherent murmur. Mr. Wingate was deeply moved. He arose and bent over her.

"Courage, my child, courage," he whispered, soothingly. "You have just started out to do the noblest work of your life. There are many years before you to live nobly and amend for the past."

"'Up, faint heart, up! Immortal life
Is lodged within thy frame.
Then let no recreant tho't or deed
Divert thy upward aim.
Shall earth's brief ills appall the brave?
Shall manly hearts despond?
Up, faint heart, up! The blackest cloud
But veils the heavens beyond.'"

These inspired lines caused Molly to raise her head. "I must command myself," she said, firmly, "for what I have to do requires courage." She arose and laid her hand caressingly upon Mr. Wingate's shoulder. "You will warn them, won't you, Silas? Keep the men from the polls. Surrender everything. Better to lose a vote than lose a life. " She moved toward the door, Mr. Wingate following. Laying her hand upon the knob, she paused and faced him. "Coming events cast their shadows before," she said. "I fear that our days of freedom are at an end in Wilming [56] ton. Good night," and Molly Pierrepont was gone. "Poor girl, poor girl," said Mr. Wingate, as he locked the door. "She might have been a queen, but, like the base Judean, she threw a pearl away richer than all her tribe.

"'Of all the sad words of tongue or pen
The saddest are these, 'It might have been.'

"Harold Carlyle's youthful life was blighted because he could not give up this woman who was unworthy of him. But at last repentance has come. God forgive her."
[57]

CHAPTER VIII.

Dr. Jose.

I will read for your consideration this evening Joshua, tenth chapter, eighth and tenth verses, which are as follows:

"And the Lord said unto Joshua, fear them not, for I have delivered them into thine hand. There shall not a man of them stand before thee.

"And the Lord discomfited them before Israel and slew them with great slaughter at Gibeon and chased them along the way that goeth up to Beth-horon and smote them to Azekah and unto Makkedah."

Thus read the pastor of one of Wilmington's Presbyterian churches at the beginning of one of the weekly prayer meetings. "Brethren," said he, "I have chosen these two verses of Scripture this evening because my mind is as, I believe, yours are—weighted down by the situation that confronts the white people of this city. No doubt all of you would like to see white man's government permanently restored, although you are most of you averse to resorting to physical force to accomplish that end. While most all Biblical students believe and teach that God told Joshua to destroy these Amorites, Canaanites and Jebusites because of their wickedness, I go further and say that they were to be destroyed because they were the black descendants of Ham, the accursed son of Noah. Joshua was commanded to utterly destroy them or put them under subjection according to God's word— 'Cursed be Canaan, servant of servants shall he be.' The Jew in this instance represented Shem, the blessed son, who was to triumph over Ham and keep him forever in subjection. God has blackened with his [58] curse the descendants of this cursed son of Noah that Shem and Japheth may ever know who the cursed of God is. You who are hesitating in doubt as whether it is right to use force to put this descendant of Ham in his rightful place—the place which God ordained that he should be—I counsel you to ponder over the passages of Scripture just read. The education of the Negro is giving him an advantage that justifies our apprehension. This, combined with accumulated wealth, make him a subject for grave and careful consideration. We are in a condition of subjection under Negro rule and domination that justifies the taking of the sword. We are God's chosen people, the banner carriers of civilization. We civilized the Negro and set him free, and it's our right to return him, if necessary, to his former condition of servitude.

"The meeting is now open for prayer, praise and exhortation." Saying this, Dr. Jose took his seat.

When the country was wrought up over the question of slavery it was the Presbyterian Church South that drafted resolutions declaring that "Slavery is a divine institution." If a divine institution, then the destruction of that institution was wrong, and the champions of freedom and the brotherhood of man open violators of divine law. If it is the will of God that the dusky children of Ham are to ever serve their brethren and ever to be reminded of their inferiority, then why not the professing Christian, the minister of the Gospel, join in the work of carrying out God's decree?

The victory of Union guns at Fort Fisher brought many carpet-baggers to Wilmington, many of them thrifty men of enterprise, who willingly assisted their brethren to restore life to that devastated town. Quite a goodly number of these good people worshipped God in Wilmington's Presbyterian Church. Therefore, among these cool and thoughtful Northerners the ministers' exhortation to retort to the shotgun was not very favorably commented upon at that meeting. But this did not in the least dampen the ardor of this hot-blooded Virginian. He went home, and instead of kneeling, as usual, by his bedside to pray, he knelt in his study. "Lord, we are sorely tried; the enemies of thy chosen people are waxing stronger and stronger. Thou art a God of [59] battle. Thou didst in days of old lead thy children to victory over the enemies. Shall we this day rise in our might? Shall we smite with the sword?" There are many instances recorded where men strong in faith have heard the voice of God assuring them of His divine approval, that He was ready to lead them to victory. But Dr. Jose heard no voice, felt no divine presence near him. He arose, took his Bible and turned again to the wars of Joshua and the terrible triumphs of Jehovah. Mrs. Jose, seeing that her husband lingered longer than usual in his study that night, glided softly in to see what so absorbed his attention. "Why do you sit up so late to-night, my dear?" she asked, softly, laying a hand gently upon her husband's shoulders. "I am exceedingly troubled to-night, Mary, darling," returned the minister. "This question of Negro Domination is troubling us. We are about to the point of desperation. Negroes are becoming so bold that our white angels are no longer safe on our streets. We have made up our minds to arm ourselves and shake off the yoke." Mrs. Jose gently closed the book and laid her hand caressingly upon her husband's head. "Cease to ponder over and keep before you the old Scripture, with its martial spirit. Remember Christ and the doctrine He came to teach. He came to teach the new commandment, to heal the broken hearted, to release the captives. 'Verily, brethren, avenge not yourselves, for it is written Vengeance is mine, I will repay, saith the Lord.' What would Jesus do under such circumstances? His was the spirit of love. He would not break the bruised reed nor quench the smoking flax. Come away, darling, and leave the regulation of everything to God." "But Mary," persisted the minister, "you don't understand the situation. We, the men of Wilmington, see utter ruin in store for us unless something is done to check the Negro. Our women can scarcely venture out alone after dark, so ugly and bold has he become under our lenient treatment." "This is all imaginary, my dear," interrupted Mrs. Jose. "I am afraid that you have allowed yourself to be influenced by these designing politicians, whose desire to gain power has stifled their love for truth. Rev. Dr. Jose is a Christian. Dr. Jose is a minister of the Gospel, who [60] should not be enticed by sinners into evil. It matters not how justifiable the deed may seem, you, my darling, cannot afford to lend either hand or voice in this contemplated work. He that taketh the sword shall perish by the sword.' Our homes, our firesides, our women are perfectly safe. The only uneasy ones among us are those who want offices. Come away, my darling; leave wickedness for the wicked to do; you cannot afford to take a hand in it." Mrs. Jose took her husband by the hand and gently led him to his bedchamber. How much happier man would be if in such trying periods of life he'd heed the counsel of the angel of his bosom. But those who read the account of the massacre of November, 1898, learned that among that body of men, who, armed to the teeth, marched to Dry Pond on that fatal morning was a minister of the Gospel. Some papers published the text which that minister of the Gospel took to preach from the Sunday following, "We have taken a city," etc.

But those hands which turned the leaves of the sacred word were crimson with the blood of the defenseless. "And Pilate took a basin of water and washed his hands before the multitude." But would we suppose that Pilate washed his hands only once? Doubtless far into the night, when the faint shouts of triumph from the enemies of God resounded through that ancient city, Pilate arose from his bed and washed his hands again, but the blood stains were still there. The court scene appears. The cry of the Pharisees rings in his ears, the humble Nazarene stands bound before him, then Calvary, with the three ghastly instruments of death upon its brow, looms up. "Out, damned spot! will these hands never be clean?" The blood stains upon his hands have doubtless worried Dr. Jose somewhat, and all the others who joined with him in the work of carnage. But the blood stains are on their hands still, and the groans and wails of innocents must ever ring in their ears. "It was a knavish piece of work." "Tell it not in Gath, publish it not in the

streets of Askelon, lest the daughters of the Philistines rejoice, lest the daughters of the uncircumcised triumph."—II Samuel, i, 20.
[61]

CHAPTER IX.

George Howe.

From the fall of Fort Fisher and political upheavals of the Reconstruction period to the awful tragedy of 1898, with the exception of a few tragic scenes, Wilmington had been the theatre of one continuous comedy, performed by gifted players, whose names and faces will ever remain indelibly fixed in the memory. Phillis, "State Mary" Tinny, George Howe, Uncle Abram, Bill Dabney, "Uncle Billy" pass over the stage before me as I write. But of those who unwittingly struggled for the foremost rank in the line of fun-making, George Howe must be the acknowledged star.

Unlike others of the same school, whose minds had become unbalanced by overwork, worry or disease, George Howe was born a fool. Being a child of honorable and respectable parentage, the playmates with whom he associated in his early youth were of that class who regarded his imbecility as a terrible affliction, were charitable and kind, never allowing others to impose upon this simple fellow, who was incapable of taking his own part. But as George Howe advanced in years he gradually threw off his stupidity, and although he never outgrew the habit of keeping his mouth open, he ceased to slobber, and acquired the habit of looking respectable. He entered school and became quite proficient in one branch of study in particular—he was an excellent reader, with a wonderfully retentive memory. But he never outgrew his simple-mindedness, and appellation of "Fool" always justly clung to him, for, bright as he seemed to be upon many things, he was incapable of applying his knowledge to his own advantage. George Howe kept abreast with the doings of the times, especially in the political and religious world, and these two subjects he was [62] always ready to discuss. Was there a public meeting called, religious, political or otherwise, George Howe would be there, often in some conspicuous place, with wide-open mouth and staring eyes, drinking in all that was said or done.

It mattered not how many were held in a single day or night, George Howe would spend sufficient time at all of them to tell something of what took place. For, with a jewsharp as his sole companion, George could cover more ground in a single day or night than any other inhabitant of Wilmington, keeping time to its discordant twanks. During political campaigns, before the press of the city could announce to its readers the result of the contest, George Howe could be heard howling the news through the streets of Wilmington. "Oh-o-o, look er here, every bod-e-e-e! New York, New Jerseee, Dilewar hev gone Dimocratic by big majoritees. Great Dimocratic gains throughout ther country. " When, in 1884, the Democratic party astonished the country and itself by electing Grover Cleveland to the Presidency by a safe majority, it was George Howe who led that host of elated Democrats down Front street and toward the Custom House on the evening of election day to inform Republican officeholders that at length their time had come to give place for others. Being generally shunned by those of his own race, George Howe cherished quite a liking for colored people, and could be very frequently found among them in their religious meetings. There was something in the Negroes' mode of worship that seemed to fascinate him, especially the saints of color who worshipped in old Ebenezer Church, in South Seventh street. When that most eloquent of pulpit orators, the Rev. William H. Banks, led his hosts to Cape Fear River's brink, and drew three-fourths of the worshippers of other denominations with them, George Howe would be there, yea, marching with the converts themselves, joining as lustily as they in the singing of that familiar old marching song:
"I'm er goin' up ter join in the army of the Lord,
I'm er goin' up ter join in the army."

Upon the river's bank he'd stand and drink in every word that flowed from the mouth of that great divine. No Negro woman or [63] man could lisp the name of "Brother Banks" with sweeter accent than George Howe, and no one could sing his praises more earnestly. Who can forget those early days of revivals and religious enthusiasm in Wilmington, and the three great divines who filled the three great pulpits from which the bread of life was given to hungry multitudes. There was Lavender in "Christian Chapel," Slubie in St. Stephen, and, more powerful and influential than either of these, was William H. Banks, the pastor of Ebenezer Baptist Church. Even years after Slubie and Lavender had been called to other fields, it was George Howe's delight to stand upon the street corner opposite the residence of the Rev. Banks and sing the parody to that famous old song that electrified and filled with the spirit the revival meetings of the early seventies:
"Brother Lavender's got some liars,
Brother Slubie's got some, too;
Jus' carry 'em down to Cape Fear River,
An' Banks'll put 'em through."
Chorus: "Git on board, children," etc.
These great men are gone into the spirit world, but George Howe still lives. Banks was the last to go, and when that coffined clay was being borne from old Ebenezer, where for sixteen years he had labored, George Howe was one of that multitude of bleeding hearts who followed his precious bones to the burying ground. He stood and looked on until the last spadeful of earth was thrown upon the coffin and the mound shaped above it. After the death of the Rev. Banks George Howe became very much attached to his eldest daughter, Mary Elizabeth, and he could often be seen leisurely strolling down Seventh street in the direction of Banks' residence, playing his jewsharp and singing the praises of "Sister Mary Lizzie" between the twanks.
"I'm er goin' down to Sister Mary Lizzie Banksies;
Sister Mary Lizzie is the daughter of Brother Banks,

An' I think er great 'eal of Sister Mary Lizzie;

Sister Lizzie, I've got ter tell you-u-u." Pausing in front of the door, he would roll up his sleeves, stretch his mouth, roll his eyes and make all kinds of comical ex [64] pressions. "Sister Mary Lizzie, I'm jus' out er jail-l-l, I'm full er lice-e-e; but jus' as soon as I take er bath I'm comin' back to see you-u-u, for I have news-s-s-s to tell you-u-u." The young lady would often have to run in and lock her doors when she'd see this harmless nuisance approaching.

George Howe was one of the few that listened to the Colonel and Teck Pervis in the Wigwam on this particular night in October. Even when the ghastly plans of the murderous clan were being discussed, no one thought of excluding the town fool, who stood gaping around taking it all in. Schults, the German, was arranging things in and about his well-filled and well-patronized grocery store on Castle street on the following morning, when George Howe entered. Grabbing a handful of dried apples from a tray which sat upon the counter, he stuffed them into his mouth, threw his long legs across a flour barrel and momentarily watched the German as he busied himself about the store. "You didn't git out las' night, Schults," said he to the German, gulping the apples down to clear his throat for conversation.

"Oudt! oudt weer?" asked Schults, pausing with a tray of onions in his hands. "To the meetin' in the Wigwam," answered George. "They done er powerful lot er plannin' there las' night. The Dimocrats mean business this time. They say they'll carry the election this time or kill every Nigger in the district. An' white men who are lukewarm, who don't come out an' take er stan' with white men will share Niggers' fate. They got the names of the lukewarm in this affair. I don't want ter skeer you, Schults, but you are on the black list." Schults had laid down the tray of onions and was eyeing George from behind the showcase. "What did you say boudt black lisdt, Gheorge?" "I say they read your name on the black list last night, an' that means they are goin' ter kill yer, for their air determin' ter kill everything in the way of white supremacy. I don't want ter skeer you, Schults; I jes' wan' ter warn you. You hain't tended eny of their meetings, and they conclude you air agin them. An' then you wouldn't discharge your Nigger." Schults' eyes flashed. He locked his hands and brought them down upon the show case hard enough [65] to break it. "What I keers fer der black lisdt, eh? I dondt keers whadt dey duse mid Schults. Before I vould hep dem ter harm dese kullod peeples py dams I suffers ter be kilt. Who ish mine frients? Who buys mine groceries? Kullud peeples. When Schults cum ster Wilmiton sick mit der rhumatiz, mit no moneys, mit no frients, who helbs Schults ter git on his feets? Dese rich bocra? No; dey kicks Schults off de sidewalks, cowhide Schults on der sthreets. Who helbs Schults den? Kullud peeples! An' befoe I rais' mine hand 'gin dem I suffer det. Let dem kum, kum an' git Schults when dey chuse. Don't let dem t'ink fur er moment I no prepare fer dem. Dem Ghermans who 'lows dem down bhroke ristocrats persuade dem gintz deir kullud frients who thrade mit dem an' keeps dem from starvin' when dese rich bocra thry ter dhrive dem frum des country deserbe de cuss ov Almighty Got! An' you damn po bocras dat allows yo'uselfs ter be make fools mit you'selfs fer broke down risterchrats ter dhrive kullud peeples frum dey homes deserfs efry one eff you' ter be kilt." George Howe's under jaw dropped. He stared at Schults in astonishment, for he did not expect to witness such a show of bravery on the part of this quiet German grocer. "I didn't mean to insult you, Schults," said he, reaching over and helping himself from a barrel of apples which stood close by. "I jes thought I'd warn you." "Now, dere's dat Gheorge Bohn," continued Schults, with apparent inattention to what George had said. "I see his nhame in der bapers as one uv der leaders in dis supremacy humbug. Who makes Bohn whadt he is on Dry Pon'? Who makes Gheorge Bohn whad he is in dis counthry? Dem very peeples who he is now thrin' ter kill. Dem broke down risterscrats, sich as Moss an' odders, cares no more fer sich as him den dey do fur de grass neat der feets. When dey gits demselfs in office dem Dutchmen kin go, po bocras kin go, dey cares noddings fur yo when dey wus rich. Now dey air po as Job's turkey, dey wants us Dutchmans an po bocras to dhrive oud our meat an' bread so dey kin demselfs git fat at de public crib. But I tells you dis: Schults will haft nodding to do mit dem. I stays in mine house, mine house is mine castle, and ef dey wants me let dem cum to [66] mine house, by dams I fills dem full uv lead; yo kin put dat in yo pipe and shmoke id." George Howe arose, yawned, then slowly walked to the door, turned, dropped his under jaw and stared again at Schults, who had resumed his work about the store. "Didn't mean ter hurt yer feelings, Schults, but ter put yer on yer giard, that unless you jine em dey air goin' ter do yo." George stepped out upon the walk, drew forth his jewsharp and sauntered up the street, twanking upon it as he went.

The German to the Southern Negro has been and is what the Jew is to the Russian peasant—the storekeeper, the barterer. The German citizen has never been a manufacturer or a farmer; he is in no business that gives extensive employment to wage earners. But, as a corner grocer, he lays for the Negro as he goes to and from his toil, and, with cheap wares and bad whisky, he grows fat upon his unwary customer. The German usually comes to this country poor, enters small towns, and, by the aid of other older residents of his nation who have already grown prosperous, he goes into business on a small scale—grocery business as a rule. He begins in a one-story structure, one-half devoted to business, while in the other he lives. These little stores were never without their indispensable liquor departments, where the trader was invited to refresh himself after paying his weekly grocery bill.

Before the war the South's best people had no use for the German emigrant, and did everything in their power to discourage his living among them. If the slave returned home to his master under the influence of liquor, the master in many instances went and cowhided the seller. The flogging of the Negro did not keep him from returning to the German to trade, and the German prospered, and to-day is among the foremost property owners in the South. I do not exaggerate when I say that the German's wealth has come to him solely through Negro patronage; not even to-day does the people known as the best people trade with Germans.

The Bohns—Joseph, Charles, George and William—coming into Wilmington in the seventies, had lived principally and conducted business in that section of the old city known as Dry Pond, and, like the most of their kind, have accumulated their wealth [67] from the patronage of the colored people, among whom they had ever lived. This makes the crime of George Bohn appear the more atrocious and cowardly. George joined the White Supremacy League during the uprising in Wilmington, and was one of its most active members. There was a certain colored citizen who knew of Bohn's secret relations to the movement which disgraced the city. This man gave the information to the people of his race who were patronizing Bohn, and entreated them not to support such an ingrate. When the excitement was at its height, when Red Shirts and Rough Riders were terrorizing the city, a band of poor whites, headed by George Bohn, sought this colored man's residence, battered down the door, fired several bullets into the bed where the man and his wife lay, the latter in a precarious condition. The house was riddled with shots; they were compelled to get out and leave their own home, to which they have not as yet been permitted to return. Bohn, after the deed was done, sneaked back to his home, and when the horrible crime was reported, tried to prove an alibi. But George Bohn is the guilty man, and George Bohn shall not escape! The hand of Justice shall point him out. His name shall go down to posterity on the list of cowards who, on the 10th of November, 1898, brought into disrepute the fair name of one of the best little cities on the American continent.
[68]

CHAPTER X.

Judas Iscariot.

When the Executive Committee, in response to Mr. Wingate's call, met in his office the following evening, the Governor's letter was read to them, and Molly Pierrepont's story repeated. Plans of action were mapped out, but not without some bitter attacks upon the enemy. Mr. Wingate's proposal to surrender for the sake of averting bloodshed, if possible, however, prevailed. The bitter language and threats made by hotheads would, if they reached the ears of whites, only add fuel to the fire already burning; so the members were cautioned by the chairman to give to the enemy no opportunity. But even among the twelve chosen of God there was a traitor, and since that memorable time nearly every band of brothers has had its Judas ready at any time of trouble to sacrifice others to save himself, or betray them for reward. Was there a Judas on the Republican Executive Committee of New Hanover county? Yes!

In the days of slavery there existed in the South a kind of Negro known as the "Good Nigger" or "White folks Nigger," who was a stubborn believer in his own inferiority and the righteousness of his enslavement. He sneaked around, grinned his way into the confidence of other slaves, then stole away and told their secrets. Were there any plots being concocted to rise up and strike a blow for liberty, the good nigger would inevitably be there to join in the shaping of plans, only to go out and hang his fellow-conspirators.

The San Domingons in their struggle for liberty found this good nigger a most formidable barrier, and those who are familiar [69] with the history of that bloody struggle know just how heart-sickening was the taking off of this creature wherever found. In many instances they cut off his toes, his fingers, his ears, his nose, stuffed pieces of these extremities into his mouth, and left him to die a slow death. The emancipation and the consequent opportunities for intellectual advancement have not changed this good nigger, for in numerous instances you will find him well educated, and often swaying quite an influence in a community. But he is generally an ignorant, shiftless fellow, forever lamenting about his freedom, flaying the Yankees for taking him away from his master, who took care of him. He still likes to sit around on the back steps of the whites' residences to talk about good old days when he was free from the responsibility of "keerin' fer mase'f." Or, in higher walks of life, from pulpit and public rostrum, he's bewailing the shortcomings of his own people and magnifying the virtues of the whites. He stands among the ashes of the victims of a mob's fury to abuse the Negro for having been killed, and to praise the whites for the crime.

George R. Shaw, a prominent negro, writes a card to the public, in which he says:

"One reason why such crimes are committed by negroes is that there is no discipline over negro children. From ten years up they are allowed to loaf about from place to place and with all kinds of characters. They have no moral restraints. Book learning in colleges dooms the negro to be fit for nothing. They think they cannot do manual labor. What my people need is an industrial, moral, common school training. Lynching does no good, and makes bad worse. The brute who will commit these crimes never sees a newspaper. Sam Hose and all such should die, but not at the hands of a mob. The negro must be taught to abhor crime from principle, not through fear. Let critics take this Sam Hose case home to themselves. If the same crime was to happen in my immediate vicinity most any of us would do very nearly like those Georgians did. If we did not lynch him we would hold the clothing of those that were doing the lynching."

Shortly after the burning of Sam Hose in Georgia, a good nig [70] ger, signing his name as Shaw sent to a certain Southern paper an article commending the action of the mob, and expressing a willingness to have held their coats while the dastardly act was performed. Did this man know that Sam Hose committed the crime for which he suffered such a horrible death? Can men capable of committing such deeds as the burning and mutilating the body of this wretch be relied upon for truth? If Cranford was one of that mob of cowards who shot to death those manacled men at Palmetto, the knocking out of his brains would have made a man of another race a hero.

Calvin Sauls, who had heretofore been a kind of an independent, having at various times voted with Democrats, Populists, Green-backers and Republicans, had shown a disposition to be earnestly interested in Republican success in the campaign of 1898. Running here and there, attending primaries and committee meetings, full of information as to the movements of the enemy, he had worked his way into the confidence of these unwary colored politicians, who considered him an earnest worker for the cause of Republicanism, so much so that he had been admitted into the headquarters of the Executive Committee on that evening. "And Judas, having received the sop, went immediately out, and it was night." No one noticed Calvin Sauls on that night, as he, taking the advantage of a moment of exciting debate, slipped out into the darkness, and made his way into the Democratic headquarters. At the corner of Fourth and Chestnut streets a dark figure stepped out from the darkness and confronted him. "Hello dar, Calvin Sauls!" said a gruff voice. "Where is you sneakin' ter? You got er few uv us fool, but not all. Goin' down ter tell wa't you foun' out at de committee meet'n, eh?" "O, g'wan way f'm me, man; I got dese white fo'ks bizness ter ten' ter." The man seized Sauls and held on to him. "Look er here, some women waited at de corner of Red Cross an' Fourth street to beat yo' las' night." "Wa' fer?" asked Sauls, trying to free himself from the man's grasp. "Fur trying ter suade dey dauters down ter dat Fayette Club for dem white mens." "It's er no sich ting!" "You lie, you louse!" exclaimed the man, loosening his hold, and shoving Sauls nearly off [71] the sidewalk. Sauls, recovering, staggered on his way.

Ben Hartright leaned against a post on the veranda of the Democratic Club's meeting place when Calvin Sauls came up. "Why hello, Calvin, is that you?" "Yes, sah, Marse Ben," returned the Negro. "I comin' ter make ma report." Ben Hartright intercepted Sauls as he placed his foot upon the door sill and drew him aside. "Say, Calvin, I saw you talking to a rather striking looking colored girl the other day; who is she? Can't you fix it so I can get an interview?" "Uh, uh," said Sauls, shaking his head. "Dat's Bob Sims' gal; she jes from college, an' she's all right now, I tell yer. You know dem Simses is top er de pot Niggers." "That's the kind I always play for, Calvin; you know me," answered Ben. "Gentlemen must always have the best, ding it all! I though you were sufficiently well bred to know that the best of everything in this world is for white people." "Dat's so," said Sauls, "but yo member dat time Bob Sims cum nie beat'n dat white man head off bout insult'n dat tudder gal er his. I feared mon." "That's all right, Calvin; I'll stand by you. Molly's gone back on me now; I'm afraid she's converted and joined the sanctified band. By thunder, she defied me the other night." "Yes, sah, an' she's in yernes', too; she's on de warpath fur true. I got er heap ter report ter night, so I see you later on dat udder matter. " And Sauls pushed past Hartright and made his way into the club room. [72]

CHAPTER XI.

Uncle Guy.

On looking over the list of Wilmingtons' personages who have been instrumental in moulding its character and making it one of the most desirable places on earth, and the memory of whose face and name revive the sweetest recollections of early youth in the dear old town, the name and face of Uncle Guy comes most vividly before me.

In ante-bellum days in the South, one week in all the year was given by the master to the slave—a week of absolute freedom, in which the Negro, unrestrained, danced and frolicked and otherwise amused himself to his heart's content. This season of freedom commenced with the dawn of Christmas, and lasted until the beginning of the New Year. The slave heard not the story of the Christ, of the wise men, or the shepherds of Bethlehem; he saw no Christmas tree brilliant with tapers even in the home of his master. For, unlike Christmas observances in the North, full of solemnity and historic significance, the Southern Christmas was and is still a kind of Mardi Gras festival, ending with the dawn of the New Year. Early on each Christmas morning the slaves, old and young, little and big, gathered at the door of the "Big House" to greet their master, who gave each in turn his Christmas "dram," and then, like a kennel is opened and pent-up hounds are bidden to scamper away, the slaves were let go to enjoy themselves to their heart's content, and were summoned no more to the field before the dawn of the New Year. While in the rural districts the frolics and kindred pleasures were the chief pastimes, in the cities and towns the celebrations were more elaborate. In gaudy rega [73] lia the "Hog Eye" danced for the general amusement, and the Cooner in his rags "showed his motions." For many years before the war Uncle Guy was the star performer at these functions in Wilmington. With whip in hand, he danced and pranced, and in sport flogged children who had been naughty during the year. But to us, who were youngsters in the seventies, Uncle Guy is most vividly remembered as a musician—a clarionet soloist—a member of the Shoo Fly Band, whose martial music will ever ring in the ear of memory.

The fall of Fort Fisher added many a new face and character to Wilmington life. Negroes who had in the conflict just closed learned of the art of war, added impetus to and stimulated the old city's martial spirit and love of gaudy display. And those who through the same agency had learned in the military bands and drum corps the art of music were indispensable adjuvants in elevating her lowly inhabitants. But he who came with the knowledge of music had a much wider field for usefulness before him; for the Negroes' love for music is stronger than love for war. Frank Johnson, who had the credit of organizing the Shoo Fly Band, had not tasted of war, but he and Uncle Guy had been "orchestra" musicians before the war. And now, as the increase of talent in Wilmington opened a wider field, the band was organized. It was called Frank Johnson's Band at first, but in after years more familiarly known as the "Shoo Fly." The name is a small matter, however; music was the chief thing. And how that band could play it! There was a ring in that music that electrified the soul and filled the limbs with renewed vigor.

There was Dick Stove with his trombone,
Henry Anderson with his bass,
Making music swift as raindrops in a race.
There was Guy Wright with his clarionet,
Henry Adams with his B,
And the music made the youngsters dance with glee.
There was Johnson, he play'd second,
Who, when horn-blowing was dull,
Could play a fiddle tempting to the soul. [74]
At Hilton, Paddy's Hollow, at the Oaks, on Kidder's Hill,
Where good and bad alike could dance their fill.
Then there was Jim, the drummer,
Who could beat a drum like Jim?
Oh! we little ones were awful proud of him.
How nicely he could keep the time.
"Shoo Fly, don't bother me!"
For I'm a member of old Comp'ny D.
It was down old Seventh to Market,
And through Market down to Third.
Playin' Molly Darlin', sweetes' ever heard;
From thence up Third to Castle, while "Up in a Balloon"
Made us wish to pay a visit to the moon.
Then we had no Gen'l Jacksons
Dressed in gol' lace all for show,
Then such hifullutin notions didn't go.
It was music! Sweetes' music!
"Darlin', I am growin' old,"
Will live, forever live within the soul.

The old Shoo Fly Band is a thing of the past; no more shall we listen to its inspiring music, for the majority of its members have crossed the melancholy flood. The last time that they appeared on the streets of Wilmington only a sextet remained. Dick Stove's trombone horn had been curtailed in order to hide the marks of decay upon its bell. They gallantly marched up Market street, and with a dismal, yet not discordant blast, turned into Fourth, en route to Hilton. I think that Uncle Guy is the only remaining one of that gallant few living in Wilmington to-day, and the friends of those who departed this life in later years followed their bodies to the grave keeping step to the sad wail of his lone clarionet. Jim Richardson, Dick Stove, Johnson, Adams, Anderson—I wonder, does he think of them now, tenderly, emotionally and with a longing to join them on the other side. I wonder if they all cluster about him when in his lonely hours he consoles himself with his clarionet. For many years Uncle Guy has been Wilmington's chief musician. Bands magnificent in equipment and rich in talent have been organized, to flourish for a few years only. But Uncle Guy's trio of clarionet and drums has [75] withstood the test of time; yea, they were indispensable for base ball advertisement and kindred amusements, heading both civic and military processions, white and black, in their outings and celebrations, or with bowed head and thoughtful countenance he has led the march to the grave. As I recollect Uncle Guy, he was the embodiment of neatness, feminine in build—it seemed that nature intended to form a woman instead of a man. Like a woman, he plaited his hair and drew it down behind his ears. His hands and feet were small, his fingers tapering; his face was black, his eyes small, his lips and nose thin, his voice fine, but harsh, and he slightly stooped or bent forward as he walked. There is poetry in every move of his bent figure as he slowly walks down the street on this autumn morning. As we gaze upon him strolling feebly along, we involuntarily sigh for the days when the heart was young. May Day, with its buds and blossoms, Christmastide, full of bright anticipations, come trooping up the misty way. We are following the old band; listen to the music! How enchanting!

"Up in a balloon, boys, up in a balloon,
Where the little stars are sailing round the moon;
Up in a balloon, to pay a visit to the moon,
All among the little stars sailing round the moon."

We are making water-mills in the brooks; we are swinging our sweethearts; we feel again the heart throbs of early youth when we dared the first caress.

"Shoo fly, don't bother me!
For I belong to Company D."

It is Monday morning—the washwoman's day of preparation; when the clothes are brought in, the shopping attended to; when the women congregate on the street corners, sit upon their baskets and bundles or lean against the fences to discuss the doings of the Sunday just past—what the preacher said and what the neighbors wore, etc. Three women stood upon the corner toward which Uncle Guy was tending. But they were not talking about texts and fashions. Uncle Guy heard the following as he drew nigh: "Bu'n um! Bu'n um! Good fer nuthin' broke down rister [76] crats an' po' white trash. Ef de men kayn't git gun we kin git karsene an' match an' we'll hab um wahkin' de street in dere nite gown." Judge Morse passed by, turned his head to catch as much as possible of what was being spoken. "Negro like," he said, as he went on his way. "They are all talk. I was raised among them, heard them talk before, but it amounted to nothing. I'm against any scheme to do them harm, for there's no harm in them. This Negro domination talk is all bosh."

Uncle Guy stepped to one side and humbly saluted Judge Morse as he

passed, then bore down upon the women who were vigorously discussing the all-absorbing topic. The old man walked out to the edge of the sidewalk, squinted his eyes and came slowly up to where the women stood, comically pointing his index finger at them: "Look yer," said he, "yuna ta'k too much!" raising his voice. "Yuna mouts g'wine ter git yuna inter trouble; hear me? Did yuna see Jedge Morse when he go by? Did yuna see 'im stop ter listen at you? Le' me tell yuna sumthin' right good. " The old man shook his finger several seconds before proceeding. "Dese white fo'kes is onter you, dey got de road all map out. Dey no ebry move yuna Nigger makin'. How dey no it? How dey no it, I say?" Another long finger shake. "Yuna Nigger uman tell um, yuna runnin' yuna tongue in de kitchen, yuna runnin' yer tongue in de street. Now, instid ov de bocra bein' in de street in dey nite gown, yuna gwine ter be thar wid nuttin on. Don't you no dat we ain't bin able ter by er gun er ounce powder in munts, an' de bocra got cannon an ebry ting. See how he'pliss yer is? Now yuna go home, an' quit so much ta'k. Keep cool fer dese bocra pisen." Uncle Guy walked slowly on and the women dispersed. Those who read the newspaper accounts of that terrible massacre know full well just how true was the prophecy of this old citizen. Doubtless he looks back over it now as a catastrophe beyond his expectations or dreams.
[77]

CHAPTER XII.

The Massacre.

The five days prior to the massacre Wilmington was the scene of turmoil, of bickerings between the factions in the political struggle; "Red Shirts" and "Rough Riders" had paraded, and for two or three days Captain Keen had been displaying his gatling gun, testing its efficiency as a deadly weapon before the Negroes.

All of these demonstrations had taken place to convince the Negro that to try to exercise his right as an elector would have a disastrous result. Upon the conservative and peace-loving these things had the desired effect. But the bolder ones showed a rugged front, and on election day hung about the polls and insisted upon exercising their rights as citizens, and many clashings were the results. But the major portion of black electors stayed at home in hope that the bloodshed which hot-headed Democrats had been clamoring for as the only means of carrying the election might be averted. When the sun set upon the little city on the 9th of November there seemed to be a rift in the storm cloud that had for so many weeks hung over it, and the city had apparently resumed its wonted quiet. Far out on Dry Pond, in the old "Wigwam" a gang of men had met, who ere the sun should set upon another day would make Wilmington the scene of a tragedy astonishing to the State and to the nation. They had gathered to await the signal to begin; they had good rifles and a plentiful supply of ammunition, and their tethered steeds standing about the old "Wigwam" were pawing and neighing for the fray. The clock in the old Presbyterian Church on Orange street dismally tolled out the hour of three. Teck Pervis arose, yawned, walked [78] up and then down the floor among the men who lay asleep with their weapons beside them. He made a deep, long, loud whistle; the men began to arise one after another, and soon the room was in a bustle. Some were washing faces, others sipping coffee as a forerunner of something hotter that would stimulate and give force to the spirit of deviltry that the work of the day required.

"Gentermen," said Teck Pervis, standing in the middle of the hall and holding a cup of coffee in his hand. "This is ther day thet ther white people of North Ca'liny is going ter show Mr. Nigger who's ter rule in Wilmin'ton, and there's ter be no drawin' back in this here bizness." Just then Dick Sands interrupted the leader by jumping out into the floor. He shuffled, he danced, kissed his gun, threw it into the air, and twirled it between his fingers like a born drum major. "Gentermen! hit's ther happies' day I seed sence way foe ther war. This is er day I bin er longin' fur and prayin' fur eber since ther ding Yanks cum and freed Mr. Nigger an' sot im on ekal footin' wid er white man. Laws er massy me'. Gentermen, I'se seed things happen in this here town sence Fo't Fisher fell thet wus enuf ter make eny dec'nt white man go inter his hole, an' pull his hole after 'im. Think uv it, gentermen, think uv it! Nigger lawyers, Nigger doctors, Nigger storekeepers, Nigger teachers, Nigger preachers, Niggers in fine houses—why, gentermen, jedgmint hain't fur off. Who was in ther Cote House thet day when thet Nigger White tole Colonel Buck he did'n no law? I wus thar, an' never wanter see sich ergin. Evrybody jis' opened his mouth an' stared fus at ther Nigger an' then at Colonel Buck. I felt thet ther merlineum wus at han', jus' waitin' ter see ther worl' turn een uppermos', an' go ter smash. Whoopalah! but we air goin' ter show um sump'n ter day, an' I jes wish thet Nigger White wus in Wilminton, fur these big Niggers'll be the firs' whose cases we'll try. Oh, Mr. Peaman, Oh, Mr. Bryant, Mr. Miller and all you uns er the Afrikin foe hundered! yo time is cum!" Dick Sands ended his harangue by turning a somersault. "I jes bet Dick Sands owes Tom Miller now," said a young chap who sat leaning against the wall with his legs spread out, laughing at Dick's Indian-like antics. "Yes," [79] broke in another; "Tom's he'ped er lot er we po' devals; he's lent out thousans er dollars in all ter white men. Hits er shame ter do him!" "Yes, I mus admit that I owe Tom, but this is er time fur me ter jump bail," said Dick Sands. "I don't b'lieve thet er Nigger should hav es much money es Tom's got no way. Hit's ergin his helth. You know Niggers liv longer po' then they do when they air rich, bekase when they're po' they air in ther natruls, an air easier kept in their places. Hit's these foe hundred Niggers thet er raisin all ther trouble." .

"Well, les git ter bizness, gentermen," broke in Teck Pervis "There's er lot befoe us ter do; Hell is ter begin at ther Cotton Press under Kurnel Moss, while Cap'n Keen'll kinder peramerlate er roun in ther middle er ther town with thet everlasting hell belcher uv his ter keep tings in check. Kurnel Wade, Tom Strong, Hines an uther big uns will sortie er roun' to'ards Dry Pond an blow up ther print'n press; thets ter draw ther Niggers out frum ther Cotton Press, so thet Kurnel Moss kin git at um, an mow em down. We uns will canter to'ards Brooklyn holdin' up Niggers as we go. Then we air to jine Hill, Sikes, Turpin, Isaacs an' others, an' raise hell in thet sexion. We uns air ter take no chances wid theese Wilminton darkies. I ain't ferget Seventy-six. Let nun git by without bein' sarched, uman er man. Shoot ef they resiss. Them's the Kurnel's orders." "Who is this man Isaacs?" asked a stranger from Georgia. "A Jew?" "Thet name's Jewey e'nuff fur yir, ain't it?" replied Dick Sands. "He is er Jew, an er good un, I tell yer. I never took much stock in er Jew, but this here un is er bo'n genterman, mo fit ter be Christun. No church in hard circumstance is ever turned away from Ole Mose; he he'ps em all, don't kere what they be, Jewish, Protestan er Caterlick, white er black. He throde his influence with ther Prohibitionists some years er go, an foute hard ter make er dry town outer Wilminton, but ther luvers uv ole ginger wair too strong an jes wallop'd ther life out er ther cold water uns. Ole Mose tuk hit cool, he died game, took his defeat like er bon fighter, bekase he'd done an fill'd his jugs an' stowd em up in de house afore ther fight begun, so he cu'd erford ter be beat. Takin er [80] drink in public was ergin his creed. Nice ole Jew tho. Keeps er paint store down street, and deals in painters' merterial, but never buys er baral er biled oil wonc't in five yers; but, like de widder in the Scripter, he alers has er baral ter draw frum when er customer wants biled oil. Ole Mose is er fine man tho; jes go in his stoe ter buy sumthin, pat him on his back, and tell him he is er bo'n genterman, an thet you b'lieve he kin trace his geneology back ter Moses an ther prophets, and thet his great-granddaddy's daddy was ther only Jew thet sined ther Dicleration of Independance; thet he looks like Napolyan, and he'll jes go inter his office an fetch yer ther fines' segyar yer ever smoked an foller yer all over ther stoe. Nice ole Jew Isaacs is. Ter see him stridin down ter bizniss ov er mawnin, yer air reminded uv ther prophets uv ole jurneyin toards Jarusalum ter read ther law." "What is the feller's name?" soliloquized a sallow-looking chap who stood with his back to the stove scratching his head in perplexity. "Name?" returned Dick Sands. "Why is you bin er listenin ter me all this time an dunno who I'm talkin erbout?" "Excuse me," returned the sallow man; "I no powerful well who yer ware talking er bout, and I wus tryin ter think uv ther name uv thet chap who's bin er stump speakin up in Sampson." "Fisher?" "No-o-o, thet ain't ther name; he's ther feller thet's runnin fur Congress." "Belden!" exclaimed several in one breath. "Thet's ther feller. Look er here," continued the sallow man, "he tole we uns up there thet ef we cum an he'p ter make Wilminton er white man's town, we ware ter jes move inter ther Niggers' houses an own em; thet's what brung me here ter jine in this here fite." "Well, I tell yer fren," answered Dick, "we air goin ter make this er white man's town, thet's no lie, but ther ain't no shoity er bout ther other matter." "Boots an saddles." Further conversation was cut off. Every man flew to his horse and the host of murderers were off in a jiffy.

The city of Wilmington was startled by the loud report of a cannon on the morning of November 10th, 1898, which made her tremble as though shaken by an earthquake. Molly Pierrepont arose, hastened to the south window of her cottage and looked out; the clouds which hung low over Dry Pond were as brilliant [81] in hue as though they hung over a lake of fire. "Tis fire!" exclaimed Molly; "the hell hounds are at their work. Ben Hartwright is keeping his word. But it's at the Cotton Press that the dance of death was to really begin, where hundreds of unsuspecting men are at work. The fire and the cannon shot are only a ruse to entice them out to be shot down. They must be warned! I must warn them!" She hastily dressed herself, locked her cottage and hurried away. Down Bladen street she hastened, turned into Fourth and across Bony bridge. At the corner of Campbell street she came upon a large body of armed men who were parleying with a negro who was making a futile protest against being searched. More than half a dozen of them thrust pistols into the helpless and frightened man's face, while two others rifled his pockets for firearms. All this Molly took in at a glance, as she hurried down Campbell street toward the press. At the corner of Third street she encountered five white boys, mere lads, who were proceeding up Campbell street. "Halt!" cried they all in one voice, and five pistols were thrust into her face. Molly paused, but with no show of embarrassment or dismay. "Come, hol up your hans!" commanded one of them, advancing a step nearer. "Hol on, fellers, we're not to search white ladies," said another, lowering his pistol, and attempting to push the others aside. "O, she's no lady; she's er nigger; I know her," returned the lad who gave the command. "Search her! tear her clothes from her! All er these nigger women are armed." The boy raised his hand to seize Molly, but was not quick enough. Molly stepped back; a quick raise of her foot sent the boy sprawling into the gutter. This completely demoralized his companions, who broke and ran. A gang of men coming up Third street inspired the boys to renew the attack upon the woman, who was hurrying on her way. "Nigger," cried the boy, raising himself up and scrambling from the gutter into which Molly's well-aimed kick had sent him. The men ran and overtook Molly, spread themselves across the sidewalk in front of her. "Will I never be permitted to reach the press?" she murmured to herself. "You've got ter be searched, ole gal," said one of the men, with a mocking smile of triumph [82] in his face, "an' you jes' es well let these boys go through them duds er your'n an' have done with it. Come now, hands up!" and they all glared like hungry wolves at the woman, who stood apparently unmoved. Molly drew herself up to her full height. "Cowards!" she shrieked. "Not satisfied at the cutting off of every means of defense from the black men of Wilmington, that you may shoot them down with impunity, you are low enough to take advantage of their helplessness to insult weak women. But here I stand!" she cried, stepping backward, and drawing a gleaming revolver from beneath her cloak. "Search me! but it must be done when the body is lifeless; I'll be a target for the whole of you before I'm searched; so let the battle begin."

The men stared at the woman in amazement. "Pluckies' Nigger gal we're tackled ter day!" exclaimed a gruff and rough-looking chap. "Got grit enough ter buil er fort. Let her go, men; not er hair un her hed mus' be tech'd!" The men stepped to one side, and Molly proceeded on her way. When she reached Front street the sight which met her gaze caused her blood to chill. From Front to Water street below was choked with armed men. To pass through such a crowd without much more difficulty was impossible. "Too late!" she sobbed. Rushing across the railroad bridge, she hastily descended the steps to the road below, crossed the tracks to the shed of the great compress, and entered by one of the large side doors. News of burning and pillage on Dry Pond had been conveyed to the workmen by another, and the news had brought confusion among them indescribable. At the main entrance to the press stood an army of whites, ready to shoot them down as they rushed forth to go to the rescue of their wives and little ones whom they thought were being murdered. White men with a cannon mounted on a lighter anchored in the river just opposite were waiting to fire upon those driven back by the fire from Colonel Moss' riflemen in Water street.

A crowd of frightened and angry men hastily retreating towards this death-trap were suddenly confronted by a woman, who like an heavenly messenger, stood with uplifted hand, her hair streaming in the wind. "Back! Back men!" she cried. "To go to the river is to be killed also; they're waiting there for the opportunity." "Molly Pierrepont!" exclaimed one of the men in astonishment. "No time for questions now!" said the woman; "your only safety from slaughter is to remain in this shed; you are not able to cope with that mob of cowards on the outside, who now are even searching women in a most shameful manner on the [83] streets. Back! Don't rush like fools to death." Molly's head began to whirl. Before any one could reach out a hand to catch her, she sank in a swoon upon the floor. Tenderly the prostrate form was lifted up, and borne to a place of safety, and an effort made to revive her. At the front entrance were huddled hundreds of negroes, cursing and crying in their desperation. On the opposite side of the street in front of a company of armed whites stood Colonel Moss, his face red with determination. Above the oaths and groans of the helpless negroes his harsh voice was heard: "Stand back, Mr. ——! I tell you again, stand out of the way, that I may blow them into eternity. " Mr. —— heeded him not, and Colonel Moss was afraid to fire for fear of injuring a British Consul. There were tears in the eyes of this good man as he went about among his angry workmen imploring them to keep cool. It was his bravery and presence of mind that prevented the ignominious slaughter of hundreds of defenseless men by a mob of armed cowards, who stood there awaiting the signal from Colonel Moss to "Blow them into eternity."

Dispatching a messenger to Dry Pond, who returned with the assurance that no one had been killed, was instrumental in cooling the negroes and inducing them to return to work. Mr. —— kept at his post until the white mob melted away to join their fellows in other portions of the city. Look! up Front Street comes an excited crowd of men and boys. Every one of them seems to be wrought up to the highest pitch of excitement. Every individual is struggling to get to some one who is in the centre of the crowd. On they come! struggling, pushing and swearing. As the mob draws near, the tall, stately figure of an old man is seen towering above them. His abundant hair and beard are shaggy and gray. He stares wildly at his tormenters, and begs them to spare his life. They shove, they kick, they slap him. "Shoot the Yankee dog! Hang him to a lamp post! Nigger hearted carpet bagger! Kill him!" Still the crowd pushes towards the depot. "Who is this man? What has he done?" asked a stranger. "Done!" exclaims a citizen close-by. '"Why he's been teachin' niggers they're es good es white men." "How long has he been in Wilmington?" "Ever sence the fall er Fort Fisher." "Is he a tax payer? Is he or has he ever engaged in any business in the community?" "Well, yes; he owns er whole county up the road there er piece." "Think of it! Bin here all these years, an' we can't make er decent white man out'n him!" "Well, [84] if he has been in this community as long as you say, and is to the community what you acknowledge, I'd like to know what right his fellow citizens have to—" "Well now, stranger, don't you think you're gettin' too inquisitive? When er white man shows that he's ergin er white man, the question of what he owns don't cut no ice; he's got ter go. This is er white man's country, an' white men are goin' ter rule it." Saying this the citizen hastened away to join the mob, who were then crossing the bridge to the depot to put the undesirable citizen upon the train to send him away.

The mob that had a few hours previous made a futile attempt to butcher the negroes at the Compress had now moved in the direction of Brooklyn like a whirlwind, sweeping men, women and children before as it went. Negroes, filled with terror and astonishment, fled before this armed mob, who shot at them as they ran.

When in a certain battle during the Revolutionary War, terror stricken colonists were retreating before the superiorly equipped and disciplined British soldiers, it was Israel Putnam who vainly implored the frightened Americans to make a stand. General Putnam cursed and swore, when he saw that it was impossible to stop his men and induce them to give battle to the British. Was there a Putnam here to essay to inspire courage into these frightened negroes, who left their wives and children at the mercy of the mob, and were fleeing toward Hillton? Yes, there was one, and his name was DAN WRIGHT. Did Dan Wright fully realize the enormity of his act as he faced this mob of white men, armed to the teeth, now pressing down upon him? Did Dan Wright feel that death was to be his reward for this act of bravery? Yes, but this did not deter him or affect the steadiness of his aim. Above the oaths and yells of this band of cowards, now almost upon him, the report of his rifle rang out, and a bandit reeled and fell from his horse. But Dan was not to escape; the crowd pressed upon him and crushed him to the earth; they riddled his body with bullets, and dragged him bleeding and torn through the streets. "Back wench!" cried a bandit, as poor Mrs. Wright pressed forward to succor her dying husband. "You shall not touch his black carcass; let the buzzards eat it!" But the mob did not tarry long beside Dan's bleeding form; they swept on to Brunswick Street, where they divided, some turning into Brunswick, while others rode toward Hillton. Dan Wright did not die in the street, however. Torn and riddled as his body [85] was, he lingered a few days in agony in the city hospital before death released him. "And the king followed the bier; and the king lifted up his voice and wept; and the king said, 'Died Abner as a fool dieth?'"

As we gaze upon the bleeding form of this simple negro, this question comes forcibly to us: Died Dan Wright as a fool dieth? Was it right for him to stand alone against such fearful odds? Yes, that the chronicler in recording this terrible one-sided fight might be able to mention one act of true bravery; that among so many cowards there was one man.

I knew Dan Wright ever since he was a lad. He was simple, quiet, unobtrusive; pious in life and glorious in death.

"He was swifter than an eagle; he was stronger than a lion." Over the humble grave in which he sleeps no shaft of granite rises to point to passers-by where this martyr to the cause of freedom lies. But when Justice shall write the names of true heroes upon the immortal scroll, she will write the names of Leonidas, Buoy, Davy Crocket, Daniel Boone, Nathan Hale, Wolf, Napoleon, Smalls, Cushing, Lawrence, John Brown, Nat Turner, and then far above them all, in letters that shall shine as the brightness of the firmament, the name of DAN WRIGHT.

Unlike most of the heroes named above, Dan's name will not in this generation be engraved upon brass or steel, or carved in marble. To an unsympathetic world he was an outlaw, who raised his arms against kings and princes, who feel that they have the sanction of God Himself to trample upon the lowly.

With tall pines as sentinels keeping watch over it, and stars for tapers tall, the body of this immortal hero lies beneath the soil enriched by his blood.
"Fleet foot on the corey,
Brave counsel in cumber,
Red hand in the foray,
How sound is the slumber!"
Who killed this simple fellow, and the score of others of his race who fell on that eventful day? The blame is laid upon the Georgians, who were invited there to assist in restoring white man's government, when there had never been any other government in existence there. But who is really responsible for this cowardly massacre? Wilmington's best white citizens, by whose invitation and under whose directions the Georgians acted. And what better market could have been sought for murderers and cowards and assassins, and intense haters of negroes than Geor [86] gia? In ante-bellum days Georgia outdid all other slave-holding States in cruelty to its slave population. The North Carolina master could subdue the most unruly slave by threatening to sell him or her into Georgia. The old negro voo-doo doctor or fortune teller could fill any negro for whom she had formed a dislike with terror, and bring him to her feet begging for mercy by walking backward, making a cross with her heel and prophesying, "You'll walk Georgia road."

When Georgia, the altar for human sacrifices, perfumed by the odor of cooked human flesh, travailed, she brought forth the prodegy of the nineteenth century, whose cries for blood would startle Catherine De Medici and cause Bloody Mary to look aghast.

Georgia bore upon her sulphurous bosom an Andersonville, within whose walls thousands of the nation's noblest sons suffered the most inhuman treatment and died the most agonizing and ignominious death. Georgia trained her cannon upon these emaciated, starved vermin-eaten creatures rather than submit to their rescue by an invading army. Georgia's convict camps of the present day are worse than slavery, and more intolerable than the Siberian mines. The order of the States upon the map should be changed so as to read as follows: North Carolina, South Carolina, Alabama, Mississippi, Louisana, Texas, Georgia, Hell. The people of Wilmington were bargaining for the genuine article when they sent to Georgia for trained murderers and assassins.

Josh Halsey was the second one to fall on that fatal day. Josh was deaf and did not hear the command to halt, and ran until brought down by a bandit's bullet. Josh Halsey was asleep in bed when the mob turned into Brunswick Street, and his daughter awoke him, only to rush from his house to death. The mob swept on over his prostrate form, shooting into private dwellings, and frightening men and children, who fled to the woods for safety, or hid beneath their dwellings.

Let us go back and see what has become of Molly. To bring her around it required heroic efforts on the part of men and the women who were the sewers of bagging on the docks. Too weak for further effort in behalf of her people, she was tenderly lifted into a buggy, carried up by way of the old Charlotte depot to her home in Brooklyn. Mrs. West, who knowing of her determination, and anxious as to her fate, had arrived at the cottage that morning too late to intercept Molly. She lingered about the cottage, however, and when they bore the exhausted and faint girl [87] home, the foster mother was frantic with grief. "It was only a fainting spell, mother," said Molly, as Mrs. West bent over her. "I was there in time to save them, but it cost me—oh so much." "You have done nobly," returned the mother, soothingly. "Your name should be placed upon the roll of honor, my dear. Go to sleep; rest serenely upon your laurels."

Dr. Philip Le Grand.

St. Stephen's Church on the corner of Red Cross and Fifth Streets, in Wilmington, is among the finest and most refined of the A. M. E. Conference. In appointing ministers to this post the most diligent care has always been exercised, for the appointee must be of the most eloquent, the most learned and efficient in the gift of the assembly. So St. Stephen's audiences have listened to some of the world's best orators, and have had the word expounded by superior doctors of divinity. Who of that great church can forget Frey Chambers, Thomas, Nichols, Gregg, Epps and others whose names I cannot now recall? St. Stephen's is among the finest of church edifices in the city, put up at a cost of over sixty thousand dollars, with a seating of twenty-two hundred. Back of her pulpit stands an immense and costly pipe organ, operated by water power, and presided over by a young woman raised up in the church, educated in the public schools of Wilmington. During the political upheaval in Eastern North Carolina, it was the fortune of Rev. Philip Le Grand, D. D. , to be the pastor of St. Stephen's, in Wilmington, and there is living to-day. Many men and women owe their lives to the wonderful presence of mind, superior tact and persuasiveness of this grave, good man. Besides being a minister, he had filled many positions of trust in the South. Yet Dr. Le Grand was both unassuming and undemonstrative. He looked for and expected a clashing of races on election day in Wilmington, but that which took place on the 10th of November was far more than he was prepared to grapple with. The dawn of that fatal day found the streets of Wilmington crowded with armed men and boys, who had sprung, as it were, by magic from the earth. Aroused by loud noises in the neighborhood of his residence, the minister arose early, dressed and hastened into the street. A large crowd of colored citizens, mostly women, stood upon the street corner half a block away, excitedly talking and brandishing broomsticks, stove-pokers, hoes, axes and other rude implements of war. All [88] was confusion among them. There seemed to be no leader, but each individual was wildly ejaculating in a manner that showed that she or he was highly wrought up. Dr. Le Grand came slowly up to them, paused and raised his hands for silence. "Why this excitement so early in the morning?" he asked. "We's prepared fer um ter day," said a woman, coming forward and brandishing a broomstick. "Dey says dey gointer kill niggers, but we's gwine ter tek er few er dem long wid us. " "Bah!" exclaimed the minister. "What will such a thing as that amount to against rifles? Disperse and go home, or you'll be sorry." This command had but slight effect upon this throng, whom Rev. Le Grand left and proceeded toward a crowd of white men and boys who stood not far distant, apparently debating the question of bearing down upon and dispersing the blacks on the corner. "Halt!" said one of the men, stepping in front of Mr. Le Grand and placing his rifle against his breast. "You can't go no further; this town's under military law now." "What means this demonstration?" calmly asked the minister, with his eyes fixed steadily upon the face of the man who had given the command. "It means that white men are in charge of things from now on," said another fellow, stepping up and eying the minister contemptuously. "You educated nigger preachers have been teaching your race that white men are not ordained to rule, and such teaching has got 'em beside themselves, so much so that the white people are compelled to take stringent measures."

"Will you kindly inform me who the leader of this movement is?" persisted Dr. Le Grand calmly. "Big words these," said the first man who had spoken. "I guess we'd better settle this nigger." "Hold on, Sam," said the second man, pushing aside the gun the man had raised. "This is St. Stephen's preacher. He is not on the list." "I'm out here in the name of peace," said Dr. Le Grand, "willing to do anything to bring that end." "Well," said the leader, producing a notebook from his breast pocket, and scribbling something in it, "we came out to-day to wash the streets in nigger gore, and if you can induce them to go home, you and others of the leading men of your race, instead of encouraging them to bully white people, you can save many lives. Colonel Moss is the gentleman to go to. But you'll need a pass," tearing a leaf from the notebook and handing it to Dr. Le Grand; "and I doubt if that will take you through the lines. You will doubtless find the colonel somewhere in the down-town section of the city. Stand aside, men, and let him pass." Dr. Le Grand took the [89] slip of paper and started for the section of the city indicated, but the way was so choked with men and boys, who challenged and parleyed with him in spite of the permit he carried, that progress was slow. Men whom he had met in his common every-day life in Wilmington, men who had been cordial and gentlemanly in their greetings, now either hurled bitter epithets at him, or passed him with averted eyes. Several times during that morning were guns pointed into his face as he paused here and there to stop collisions that were constantly occurring between white and black men, fatal in every instance to the blacks, who, without arms, were no match for the well-equipped whites, who took advantage of their helplessness to bully them. The most thrilling scene witnessed was that which made the minister's heart faint, although the incident excited the admiration of all who beheld it. Above the oaths of excited men and boys was heard a wild cheer a few blocks away, followed by the defiant cry of a negro boy, who came panting up the street, unmindful of the cry of "halt" that issued from many lips. Frantically waving a huge revolver in his hand, he fell upon his face within a few yards of where the minister stood, pierced by a rifle ball. Turning over slowly upon his back, he leveled his pistol and fired into the crowd of men closing in on him, shattering the arm of a Georgia bandit. "He is dying!" exclaimed the minister, with uplifted hand to prevent the men from doing further violence to the dying lad, whose lifeblood was making crimson the sand where he lay. One man in the crowd stooped and picked up the pistol that had fallen from the lad's grasp. He raised it up before the crowd and said: "Let him die in peace, boys; I admire a brave heart, if it is under a black skin." The crowd dispersed. The minister got down upon his knees and raised the lad's head into his arms. He opened his eyes and fixed them upon the face of the man of God, who had begun to stroke his forehead with his hand. "God be merciful to thee, my son," said the minister tenderly. "Dat's all right, parson," returned the lad faintly, with a smile upon his ebony face. "I tol' um I'd die foe I'd giv' up ma gun, an' I tink dat when I tun ober dat time I got one er dem."

"What is your name, my son?" asked Dr. Le Grand, eagerly. There was no answer; the boy was gone into undying life. The minister gently laid the little hero back upon the ground to await the arrival of the undertaker's wagon, and went on his way. This incident somewhat awed the bandits, some of whom stood off some little distance and watched him through the scene; and [90] his progress was attended with but little further difficulty. When he reached Front Street, however, the Record Office on Dry Pond had been burned, and the futile attempt to murder the workmen at the cotton press had been made. Several black men had been killed during the morning, and their bodies left where they had been shot down. At the corner of Front and Chestnut Streets three men passed him under guard, walking rapidly toward the depot, and whom he recognized as prominent citizens—one a grocery man another quite an extensive real estate owner and money lender, while the third, a white man, had been a magistrate in the city for quite a number of years. These men were being escorted to the trains by soldiers, who had considerable trouble in keeping a mob of men and boys from doing them violence. "Well, what are you standing up here for?" asked a man, turning aside from the throng that surrounded the fugitives, and akimbowed in front of the minister. "No niggers are allowed to loiter; white men are in charge of affairs from now on." "I have a pass that permits me to interview the Colonel," answered Dr. Le Grand, holding up the paper before the man's eyes. The man took the paper and read it slowly. "Come," said he in a gentler tone of voice, "I'll take you through to the Colonel, for you can't go by yourself." Across the street, and in the direction of the cotton press they proceeded. At the corner of Mulberry Street they met Colonel Moss going southward, with a crowd of soldiers and citizens about him. He scowled at the minister, his face flushed with anger as the minister saluted. "What do you want?" he roared. "That's the question I have come to ask you," returned the minister. "What do you wish us to do? We are willing to do anything to stop this carnage." "We want nothing! We are masters of the situation," answered the Colonel hotly. But the minister persisted. "Hear me, Colonel. This is indeed a one-sided fight. Our men are unarmed, and are the chief sufferers in this affair." "It's your own fault," roared Colonel Moss. "We gave you colored leaders time to comply with our request to burn the negro's printing outfit. We waited twelve hours for your reply, and it came not, so we took the matter into our own hands. We propose to scourge this black pest out of Wilmington. If you can induce them to go to their homes and recognize the authority of the white people, you can prevent further bloodshed." "I will do my best," replied the minister. Dr. Le Grand was placed in a buggy, between two whites, to protect him against violence. This man of God finished that day, [91] and the other days of terror to the unfortunate negroes, in inducing rebellious black citizens throughout the city to submit to overwhelming odds against them, and staking his own life upon the good character of this or that man or woman in danger of being killed for some trivial charge made by a white person, whether remote or recent. [92]

CHAPTER XIII.

Mrs. Adelaide Peterson's Narrative.

New Bedford, Mass., Dec. 19, 1899.

Dear Jack Thorne:

In compliance with your request for a narrative of what I witnessed of the massacre which took place in Wilmington, N. C., in November, 1898, I herewith write for the information of the world what happened in the section of the city known as Dry Pond. The plans for the slaughter of November 10th had been carefully laid. The negroes, lulled into a feeling of security by the usual yet unexpected quiet election, were utterly surprised on the morning of the 10th to find the streets choked with armed men and boys. The mob, it seems, formed at the Court House, and dividing itself into bands scattered into every direction, holding up and searching both black men and women, beating and shooting those who showed a disposition to resist. On the corner of Seventh and Nun Streets stands Gregory Normal Institute for colored youth, with Christ Church (Congregational) and the teachers' home, comprising the most beautiful group of buildings in the city. This is the property of the American Missionary Association. The morning devotions had just ended in this school on the morning of the 10th, and scholars were going to the different class-rooms, when the report of a gun threw the entire school and neighborhood into confusion. Children ran to their teachers for safety, who, with blanched faces, stood dumb with terror, for a mob of armed whites had already surrounded the buildings and completely blocked Seventh, Ann and Nun streets. On Seventh street, between Nun and Church streets, in a small wooden structure, the much talked of *Wilmington Record* had found a temporary home, and this was the objective point of the mob. Surrounding this building, they battered down the door, broke in pieces the printing outfit, and then set fire to the building. Many women, with their little ones, took to the woods, [93] so thoroughly frightened were they at this strange and unlooked-for spectacle. Black men were awed into helplessness by the superiorly armed mob. I was at the ironing table, when one of my little ones ran in and told me that the school house was on fire. I hurried out to join the crowd of anxious mothers, who were hurrying in that direction to rescue their children, whom, they supposed, were in danger. But we were not able to get past the crowd of men who surrounded the Record building. The cries of the frightened children could be heard, and the inability of the mothers to reach them added to the horror of the scene. One mother, frenzied with grief and desperation, pushed and shoved her way through, despite the threats of the mob. One little girl died of sheer fright. The shooting without, mingled with the oaths of the men and the frantic wails of the women without were too much for the little one to bear. Her teacher's assurance of safety were of no avail. The teachers finally made a bold front, pushed their way through the crowd and delivered the frightened children to their frightened parents, some of whom did not return to their homes, but hastened to the woods for safety. I returned home. My husband, who worked at the Press did not arrive until late that night, he having had serious difficulty in passing the armed whites who lined the streets, and challenged him at every corner. He informed me that Colonel Moss, on leaving Dry Pond, went immediately to the Press with the intention of killing all the men at work there, but was thwarted by the coolness of Mr. —— and Molly Pierrepont, who went from her home to warn them. I bless that woman for her courage. She stood like a goddess among those men and prevented them from rushing into a trap prepared for them. My husband at first thought it unsafe to remain in the house that night; the poor whites were heavily armed and were likely to do most anything. They had already fired into several houses in the neighborhood. Some one rapped at the door. I was too frightened to move. My husband finally opened the door, and in staggered Joe Bently, bleeding profusely from a large gash in his forehead. He said: "I was trying to reach the hill this evening without being searched, as I did not want to part with my gun. At the corner of Market and Front streets I met Mr. Philip Hines, who offered to take me through the crowd to safety, and led me right into trouble. I was held up and searched. Ben Turpin took my revolver from me and gave me this gash on my forehead with the butt of it." I bathed and bound up Bently's wound, and he [94] lay himself upon the lounge in my dining-room, and being weak from the loss of blood, soon dropped off to sleep. We were too frightened to lie down. Thirty minutes elapsed. We heard the sound of footsteps approaching; the door received a vigorous kick. "Hello!" came from without. "Say Peterson! Don't be afraid; this is McGinn!" My husband opened the door. "Is that you, Mr. Mac?" said he. "Yes, we are looking for that feller Manly." "I guess he's far away," returned my husband. "Well, its good for him that he is. Who's in there with you?" "My family." "Well, I believe you, Peterson. Good night." The men went their way. We were molested no more during the night, but shooting was kept up at intervals in the neighborhood all night. Some citizens slept under their houses for safety.

The morning of the 11th of November dawned clear and cold, and the sufferings of those who were compelled to sleep in the open air were terrible. At about nine o'clock Rev. Simons called at my house. He had his wagon laden with comfortables for the suffering ones. "Hundreds are in the woods," he said after greeting me, "and God only knows what their sufferings were during the night."

"People of the Saxon race, whom we have trusted so implicitly, this is your work, for which you must answer to God," and with his hand he brushed away a tear. Together we rode to the woods, my husband remaining home with the children. Far beyond "Jump and Run" we came upon quite a crowd of women and children, who had built a large fire, and were huddled about it. One woman, a tall creature, ran to meet us as we approached with outstretched hands and a maniacal stare in her eyes. "Where's my husband?" she shrieked. "Is it true he is killed? An' are you comin' to kill me?" "No, my dear," answered the minister, "we come to bring you comfort." "No! no! no!" she cried. "Tell me no more about God. Hagar's children have no God. They are forsaken! Lost! lost! lost!" Several women came up and took hold of the demented creature and led her away. "She's los' her mind," said one. "She sat here las' night an' saw her dear friend an' neighbor die in the agony of childbirth; and that, with the news of her husband's death has unbalanced her mind." "There lays the woman," said another, taking the minister by the hand and leading him to where—cold and lifeless—the body of the woman with that of the new-born babe by its side. The poor, demented creature had taken a seat upon a stump beside the corpse, and was moaning and wringing her [95] hands. "Lord, be merciful!" exclaimed the minister, with clasped hands. "They are all about here," said another woman; "these are not all that have died during the night." We busied ourselves in giving such comfort as lay in our power. In our search among the bushes we came across several dead and others dying from the night's exposure. So thoroughly frightened were these people that we could not induce them to believe it safe to venture back to their own homes. The situation was indeed appalling. On our way into the city we met some humane whites going out to persuade the frightened refugees back.

The 10th day of November, 1898, can never be forgotten. I will not close this narrative without mentioning an act of bravery performed by a lone woman which stopped the vulgar and inhuman searching of women in our section of the city. The most atrocious and unpardonable act of the mob was the wanton disregard for womanhood. Lizzie Smith was the first woman to make a firm and stubborn stand against the proceeding in the southern section. It was near the noon hour when Lizzie, homeward bound, reached the corner of Orange and Third streets. A block away she saw a woman struggling to free herself from the grasp of several men who were, in turn, slapping her face and otherwise abusing her. The woman fought until her clothes were torn to shreds; then with a shove the men allowed her to proceed on her way. Lizzie could have saved herself by running away, but anger at such cowardice had chased away every vestige of fear. She leisurely walked up to where the fight was going on. "Halt," said one of the ruffians to Lizzie, "an' let's see how many razors you got under them duds. That tother wench was er walkin' arsenical. Come now!" roared the man, "none er your cussed impert'nence." Lizzie, instead of assaying to comply, akimbowed and looked defiantly at the crowd about her. "Oh, yo' po' white trash." "Shut up or we'll settle you an' have done with it," said the leader, making a motion toward his hip pocket. "Yo' will, eh!" answered the girl, "yo' kan't skeer me. But ef yo' wanter search me I'll take off ma clothes, so yo' won't have ter tear 'em," and Lizzie began to hurriedly unfasten her bodice. "Yo've got ter search me right," she continued, throwing off piece after piece; "yo'll fin' I am jes' like yo' sisters an' mammies, yo' po' tackies." "That'll do," growled one of the men, as Lizzie was unbuttoning the last piece. "Oh, no," returned the girl, "I'm goin' ter git naked; yer got ter see that I'm er woman." White women were looking on from their windows at this sight so [96] shocking. One had the courage to shout "Shame! how dare you expose that woman in that manner?" "Them's the curnel's orders," replied the leader, raising his hat. "Who is the Colonel, and what right has he to give such orders?" shrieked the woman. "You ought to be ashamed of yourselves for your own wives and daughters' sakes." The men skulked away and left Lizzie victor on the field. Yours for justice and right,

ADELAIDE PETERSON.

[97]

CHAPTER XIV.

The Flight of Reverend Selkirk.

There is a great deal said about the fatality of the wind of Boston Bay. Even the native Bostonian dreads its icy touch, and when winter comes to re-enforce its intensity, as many as can, seek warmer climes. A few winters ago, among the many tourists who sought accommodations on a train South-bound were Rev. Hiland Silkirk, wife and two children. Rev. Silkirk's many years of ministerial work in the old cradle of liberty had somewhat told upon his health, and he felt that a few months or years in a warmer clime would result in the recovery of lost vigor. He had purchased a ticket for Wilmington, N. C. The air there was mild, bracing and dry and made health giving and mellow by the sweet odor of the yellow pine. And then, again, a field was open for the continuance of his work while he recuperated, a certain Baptist church in the old city had called him to its pastorate. Being a man of exceptional ability, affable and of sunny temperament, Rev. Hiland Silkirk was just the man to win friends among Southern people, and he won them among both white and black citizens in that old town. This is the case in every Southern community. A Negro man of prominence can retain his popularity on certain lines among the whites if he keeps out of politics and in all race troubles remains neutral. But he cannot take this stand and be universally loved. His reward will inevitably be the contempt of his own race, which he cannot afford to engender. And no man who loves his people can hide his light under a bushel; can keep quiet when they are assailed. He must, he will raise hand and voice in their defense. Moses refused to dwell in the king's palace while his people suffered about him. No! he went forth, and in his zeal smote an uncircumcised Egyptian oppressor to death and fled into a strange land and there fitted himself for their deliverer. Rev. Hiland Silkirk counted his friends among some leading ministers and laymen of the oppo [98] site race. But Rev. Silkirk was true to his own, and when the time came to test that devotion, he arrayed himself with his own people and endangered his own life. When, in the early part of August, 1898, the fight between the editor of the Record and the editor of the Messenger waxed hot over the inflammatory letters on the race question from the pen of Mrs. Fells, of Georgia, which had its final result in the destruction of the Record's property and the banishment of its editor, Rev. Silkirk did not hesitate to join in the controversy. This caused many of his white friends to cool towards him, and it placed his name upon the list of dangerous(?) Negroes to be killed or banished. After the general raid which terrorized and put the city in a state of panic on the 10th of November, the mobs divided into squads, and, as deputy sheriffs, begun to arrest and drive from the city the objects of their spleen. The duly elected Mayor and other officials having been deposed, bandits were put in their places. A portion of the mob which destroyed the Record building on the morning of the 10th, started northward toward Walnut street, on which the hated Negro minister resided. But among the white ministers in Wilmington there was one at least who would not allow his prejudice to impair his devotion to a worthy friend. He, aware of the plot to murder the black divine, set out on that morning to warn him of his danger. The Rev. Silkirk, aroused and alarmed by the noise of guns coming from every direction in the city, had just mounted his bicycle and started in the direction of Dry Pond. As he turned into Seventh street he saw, more than two blocks away, another bicyclist breathlessly pedaling toward him. "Why, Dr. Sawyer, I was just starting to your house!" said the colored man, as the white one rode up and dismounted. "And I was just coming to your house to inform you that a ride in my direction is dangerous! Return! There is no time to be lost. Get into the woods! They are on the way to your house now to kill you. I must not be seen with you.

Go! Make haste!" This was all said in one breath, and before the colored man could recover from his astonishment to ask a question the white one was gone. Down the street a cloud of dust rose before the colored minister's eyes. The bandits were only a few blocks away. There was not even time to return to his home. He hastened down Walnut street, crossed Red Cross into Campbell, and made for the woods. The bandits rode up to the minister's house, dismounted and surrounded it, but the quarry was gone. From the frightened wife and little ones they could glean no information as to the where [99] abouts of the minister. They were about to satisfy their vengeance by subjecting the helpless woman to revolting indignities, when a boy ran up to inform them of the direction in which the man had fled. The mob mounted their horses and made a dash for Oak Dale Cemetery. The colored people in the neighborhood, afraid to approach to offer protection to poor Mrs. Silkirk, now gathered about her. All were unanimous in the belief that the bandits would return should they fail to find the minister, and not only molest her, but shoot into the houses of others as well. So they decided to take her to the church, yea, gather the whole neighborhood in there. "Sho, dey won't shoot in de house er God," said an old lady. "Le'us git dar an' pray; we kin do nuth'n better. Le' us ask de Lawd wot it all means?"

When Rev. Silkirk reached a secluded spot in the woods he was wet, sore and exhausted from wading through marshes and being scratched by briars. Night had set in. He lay down beneath a clump of bushes to rest; but there was no rest for this poor innocent wretch, outlawed by ruffians and compelled to leave his wife and little ones, and be hunted as a wild beast in the forest. This is the fate of many a Negro who had committed no more offense against law and order. But this, to such characters as Rev. Silkirk, was no evidence of God's displeasure. Men more righteous than he had been compelled to flee for their lives; yea, suffer death for truth's sake; men of whom the world was not worthy. He pillowed his head upon a tuft of wire grass, and gazed upward towards the spangled skies. "Lord, we cannot tell why this, thy people, are so severely tried; yet we believe that all things work together for good to them that trust in Thee. Strengthen our faith, Lord. Save our wives and little ones from a fate worse than death at the hands of the wicked, who glory and take delight in shameful treatment of the defenseless. " He heard the tramping of horses' feet among the bushes only a short distance away, and soon several men galloped past where he lay—so close that one of the horses brushed against the bush which sheltered him. The frightened minister lay perfectly still until the footsteps died away, then he arose and went cautiously back to the city to see, if possible, what had been the fate of his wife and children, left to the mercy of a disappointed and angry mob.

The feeling that the church was the only place for safety filled the breasts of most of the frightened souls in the neighborhood of Seventh and Red Cross streets on the evening of the dreadful 10th of November, after the band of Red Shirts had terrorized the [100] people in their blusterous hunt for the negro minister. "It seemed like the day of Judgment," said an eye witness. "There were no loud lamentations, as is usual when colored people are wrought up under excitement, but sobs, groans and whispered petitions. Bless our pastor, Lord, an' save him ef it be Thy will," came from many lips, followed by "Amens" and "Do, Lord." Suddenly the church was thrown into a spasm of excitement that could not be suppressed, for while they were breathing prayers for his deliverance, the pastor, wet, footsore and tired, entered and strode slowly up the aisle. "Why did you, oh, why did you come back?" exclaimed his wife, throwing her arms about the minister's neck, while others in their excitement gathered about them. The Rev. Silkirk gently led his wife, who had almost fainted in his arms, to a chair and raised his hand for silence. "Brethren and sisters," he began, "my escape from death to-day has been a narrow one. I knew that my attitude in the Manly-Fells controversy had caused some of my friends to cool toward me, but I did not believe that it would ripen into a desire to murder me, because of my opinions. Nevertheless, my attitude is the same. I do not retract a single word said in defense of my people. Twenty or more men were killed to-day—men who are innocent of any wrong. I may be numbered with them before morning; yet love for my wife and little ones and you caused me to tempt death by returning here to console and speak a word of comfort to you. These may be evidences of God's displeasure; we may have in our prosperity forgotten to give Him the glory due unto His name; yet by these afflictions we may know that we are beloved of God, for whom he loveth He chasteneth. We are too well schooled in affliction to be dismayed, and they who are responsible for this rioting may just as well try to stop the river in its flow as to try to triumph permanently over a people who by affliction have waxed so strong in faith. We are as firm as Mount Zion, which cannot be moved. You, all of you, deem it expedient that I go away; so to-night, by the help of the Lord, I shall try to get away from this place. I may see you again, I cannot tell; if not, there are twelve gates to the City, and, with God's help, we'll meet up there. Let us have a few moments of silent prayer." Every knee was bended on that terrible night; but so emotional is the colored American that silence in a meeting of this kind is maintained with difficulty. A silence of two minutes elapsed—followed by sobs and groans painful to listen to. Then a voice tremulous with emotion floated over the assemblage—a woman's voice:

[101] "Father in heaven, we have evidence that thou didst hear thy children's cry in days past and gone, and we believe that Thou wilt hear us now. (Yes, Lord.) Thou didst hear the Hebrew children. (Yes.) Thou didst deliver Daniel. (Yes.) Thou didst hear Africa's groans, and didst break her chains. (Yes, Lord.) Oh Jesus, Master, hear us to-night. (Do, Jesus.) We cannot tell,

Lord, why we are buffeted, beaten, murdered and driven from our homes, and made to seek refuge among strangers; but Thou knowest. Perhaps in our prosperity we have forgotten to give Thee the glory, blessed Lord, and these demons that have flocked to Wilmington from all quarters may be the scourgers that Thou art using to bring us closer to Thee. Hear, O Lord, the groans and cries of the widows and orphans of the slaughtered ones; men who gave up their lives in the feeble efforts to defend their homes and firesides. (Do, Lord.) Bless Brother Silkirk and his little family (Amen), who are about to start upon a perilous journey. The way is beset by demons thirsting for his blood. (Lord, help.) But he's in Thy hands, and Thou canst save him and save us from further persecution, if it be Thy will. Amen!"

Rev. Silkirk was visibly moved by this earnest and pathetic plea. He thanked the petitioner and the entire church for their solicitude. He was dissuaded from attempting to take his wife and little ones with him on his perilous journey, and they were left in care of friends until an opportune season presented itself. The parting between that good man and his wife and friends was indeed touching. A substantial bank note was hurriedly thrust into his hand, and, with two deacons, he stepped out into the darkness and disappeared.

When the North-bound passenger train leaving Wilmington at 12.01 slowed up at Castle Hayne on the morning of the 12th of November a wretched-looking Negro minister stepped aboard. The trains had for two days been leaving the city ladened with undesirable citizens, white and black, and the trainmen had been earnest abettors in the injury and insult offered them. From Wilmington to Weldon at every stop crowds waited to do injury, if possible, to "Nigger" and radical refugees. Thomas Miller, Aria Bryant and other citizens had been taken off and jailed at Goldsboro, and one man in trying to escape was shot to death.

The Rev. Silkirk did not feel very comfortable under the searching eye of the conductor who lifted his fare, and that individual's [102] refusal to give satisfactory answers to inquiries concerning connections at Rocky Mount increased his feeling of uneasiness. He felt assured that failing to capture him in the woods, his would-be murderers had telegraphed his description, etc., along the road. At Dudley Station two men came into the smoker and took seats immediately in front of him, and continued the discussion of the topic which doubtless absorbed their minds before entering. "I was saying," said one, an elderly man, with quite a refined appearance, "that impertinent article by that Negro preacher was equally as spicy as the editorial, and as the editor took time by the forelock and made good his escape, the determination was to make sure of this preacher. But he was warned in time to get out, and the impression is that he was warned by a white man." "Shame," said the other, slapping his knee vigorously. "He got away, then." "Yes, but it's likely he'll sneak back before taking final leave, as he has a family there, and they are on the lookout for him; besides, the boys have been notified along the road to be on the lookout." "What's his name?" "Silkirk; he is er Boston darkey, an' doubtless is heading for that place, as Southern climate has got too hot for 'im."

"Goldsboro! Change cars for Newbern," shouted the porter. "Well, good-bye!" said the genteel man, rising and making a bolt for the door. As the train slowly clanged its way through the old town the remaining passenger settled himself back in the seat and went to sleep.

Several men passed through the train, the conductor in the lead. Each man slyly glanced at the minister, but said nothing. The train sped on its way through the town.

Now, Wilson is the place where through passengers change cars and board North-bound trains from the far South. Wilson for the past few days had been the rendezvous for a well-organized vigilance committee, who had vied with the ruffians at Goldsboro in offering violence to citizens driven out of Wilmington. The leader of this gang was a young farmer by the name of Bull. That afternoon Mr. Bull and quite a number of his fellow-committeemen sat on the steps of the railroad station whittling sticks when the station operator came up and handed him a telegram, which ran as follows: "Goldsboro—Man on train 78 answering description of Silkirk. Look out for him. Barnet."

"By Joe!" exclaimed Captain Bull, jumping to his feet. "Well, what's up?" asked three or four of his companions, gathering around the leader. "Nothing, only that Boston black Yankee is [103] on train 78, an' he mustn't git any further 'an Wilson, that's all," returned Bull. "Go, Buxton," he said to a sallow-faced young man leaning against the wall, "an' tell the boys ter git ready for er feast ter night. That Nigger editor slipped through like grease, an' ef we let this Nigger do so we all uns ought ter be gibbited. We want er be ready ter mount the train time she stops. I've got no description of the man, but, then, its no hard tas' to pick out er preacher from the tother uns." With that Captain Bull started toward home to get his gun, and the crowd dispersed.

At Wilson trains usually pause at the water tank, a few yards below, for coal and water, before making the final stop at the station. Just as train 78 paused at this place, a colored man with a buggy whip under his arm got aboard. He walked briskly through the train, scanning the faces of the passengers as he went. "The' ain't but one colored man on here," he said, as he reached the door of the smoking car and looked in. Walking up and touching this man on the shoulder, he said: "Looker here, mister, you goin' North?" "I want to," returned the colored passenger. "Well, come with me an' get somethin' ter eat foe you go; you look like you hungry. I keep er resterant, put up thar jes' fer my people, bekase thar's no show fer 'em in the other place. Come on! No time ter be los', train don't stay up thar more 'an twenty minutes." With that he led the passenger from the train. "Git up in thar," he said, pointing to a small wagon. "Got er trunk?" "No, just this bag," returned the other. "Well, let's go.

Git up, Nell," and the horse started off in a brisk trot. "Looker here, mister, I ain't got no more resterant then er dog. Ain't your name Silkirk?" "That's may name," returned the passenger in astonishment. "I knowed it," said the driver. "I got on that train ter save yer life ter night. Slower dar, Nell! This road's full er mud holes sence the big rain we had tother day. I jes' happen ter that depot ter day jes' in time ter see thet telegraph when hit cum an' was put inter Captain Bull's han'. Sence dem riots in Wilmin'ton he's bin er getin' telegraphs an' sarchin' trains, an' insultin' women an' killin' col'd mens. An' I jes' slied erroun' tell I hear what that telegraph say. Hit say, look out fer Silkirk. Thar's er gang of crackers waitin' ter kill you as sho es yo' er bo'n; but Bob Jones is goin' ter cheat um dis time. Go on thar!" "God moves in a mysterious way," murmured the minister, slowly. "You'll bet he does. Come, gal, pick um up an' put um down; thar's no time ter be los'. Gwine [104] ter take yer cross de country here, an' put yer on er frate train, an' dat train gwine take yer to Norfolk, for yo' sholy ain't safe on dat coas' line road. Dis is what we call throwin' de houn's off de scent. Pure Nigger cunnin', here me? Git up, Nell."

It was near the midnight hour when the horse, panting for breath, paused at a lonely rickety old station. The men alighted. "Hit's jes' twenty minutes pas' eleven," said Bob Jones glancing at his watch. "Now that train's comin' long here in er few minutes. Jes' git er board an' treat de Cap'n right, an' he'll put yer through." "God bless you and all of yours," said the minister, gratefully. "My people in Wilmington and Boston must know of you and what you have done for me to-night." "Dat's all right, parson, keep de change. Ise jes' doin' my duty, that's all. We should feel each other's keer, an' bear each other's cross, says de good word. Dar's de train now!" The old freight train panted slowly up and stopped to look for freight. The Rev. Hiland Silkirk, with tears of gratitude in his eyes, got aboard, and the triumphant Jehu turned his horse and started homeward.

"Well done, good and faithful servant, forasmuch as you have done good unto one of the least of these my brethren, you have done it unto me." [105]

CHAPTER XV.

Captain Nicholas McDuffy.

Before the introduction of the improved method of fire fighting in Southern cities—before the steam engine, the hook and ladder and water tower companies supplanted the old hand pump and bucket companies, the Negro was the chief fire fighter, and there was nothing that tended more to make fire fighting a pleasant pastime than those old volunteer organizations. For many years after the war Wilmington was supplied with water for the putting out of fires by means of cisterns which were built in the centre of streets. When the old bell in the market house tower sounded the alarm of fire, the volunteers left their work and hastened to headquarters to drag forth the old hand pump and make for the cistern nearest the scene of the fire, where, keeping time to the tune of some lively song, they pumped the fire out. There was peculiar sweetness in those old songs which made fire fighting a fascinating pastime in those old days. While a few men spannered the hose, directed the stream and did the work of rescuing and saving furniture, etc., the majority were required to man the pumps. Thirty or forty men in brilliant uniform lined up on either side of the huge engine, tugging away at the great horizontal handles, presented a spectacle which no one even in these days of advancement would despise. And the singing!
"O Lindy, Lindy my dear honey,
Lindy, gal, I'm boun' to go;
O Lindy, Lindy my dear honey,
O Lindy, gal, I'm boun' to go," etc.
A few lines of another:
"The cows in de ole field, don't yo' hear de bell?
Let her go, let her go.
The cows in de ole field, don't yo' hear de bell?
Let her go, let her go," etc.
[106] But the things that will make those old organizations live longest in the memory are their frolics, excursions and picnics, full of all that appealed to the appetite for pleasure and excitement. There the dancer, the fighter, the runner, the wrestler, could indulge freely in his favorite pastime; there old scores could be settled and new ones made. The most noteworthy and serviceable of those old volunteer organizations was the old "Brooklyn No. 4," which guarded that portion of the city known by that name. No. 2, in the middle section, and the "Old No. 3 Double Deck," in the southern part of the city. These old-fashioned machines have given place to the modern fire fighter, the steam engine. But of all of these banished organizations, No. 3 will be the longest remembered. Upon her roll were the names of some of Wilmington's best citizens. In the year 1873 this company, too serviceable to be disbanded, was reorganized under the name of "Cape Fear Engine Company," and presented by the city with a handsome steam engine of that name. And although the Germans had replaced their hand pump by costly steamer, and a company had been organized among the aristocracy, this colored company kept and maintained the reputation of being the best fire fighters in the city, and second to none in the entire State. Upon the walls of their engine house hung trophies for superior firemanship won in nearly every city in the State. The insurance companies of the city recognized their value as savers of property, and upon more than one occasion made them valuable presents. Only men of good repute who could "stand the gaze of an honest eye" were eligible to membership in the Cape Fear Fire Company, and he who aspired to leadership must be efficient both in character and experience as a fire fighter. I write the above that the reader may know what manner of man this was who was compelled to leave his home, his wife and little ones and flee for his life. Captain Nicholas McDuffy was at one time foreman of the Cape Fear Engine Company. McDuffy came to Wilmington a rough country lad, secured employment, went

to work, saved his money, bought property and became a citizen of note and respectability. He joined the engine company and rose like a meteor to its foremost rank. The relations between the races in the South have always been such that it requires a Negro of Spartan courage to face a white man and return blow for blow, it matters not how righteous may be his cause. Captain Nicholas McDuffy was a man without fear. Two or three years ago, while a member of the police force of Wilmington, it became his duty [107] to arrest some white roughs for disorderly conduct. It was a hazardous undertaking, but McDuffy waded in and landed his men, but it cost him dear. His body was so hacked by knife thrusts that he was compelled to go to the hospital for repairs. Generally policemen are commended and rewarded for such heroic deeds, but this placed the name of Nicholas McDuffy upon the death list. A Negro officer must not presume to arrest a white man. There were, however, white men who admired McDuffy for his frankness and courage, and when the riotous excitement was at its height and the assassins were seeking here and there for victims, one of these true men warned McDuffy just in time to get into the swamp before a mob surrounded his house. They pursued him, however, but by swimming a creek not far from the city's limit he escaped their bullets, and without coat or hat made his way to New Berne. His poor wife and children were left to the mercy of the mob, who drove them forth and burned the house behind them. [108]

CHAPTER XVI.

Tempting Negroes to Return.

Wilmington Officials Scouring the Woods for Refugees—Want Them to Return and Go to Work.

Special to The World.

Wilmington, N. C., Nov. 13.—Affairs are settling down to their normal condition here. Chief of Police Edgar G. Parmle and several representatives of the new city government drove out ten miles on the various roads leading from the city to-day, to induce the refugee Negroes to come back.

City officials also attended the colored churches and urged the pastors and their people to go into the woods to induce the frightened Negroes to return and resume their work.

The pastors of the white churches referred to the riot in their sermons to-day. The burden of the discourses was that the struggle at the polls Tuesday was for liberty, decency, honesty and right; that it was not so much the drawing of the color line as a contest for the supremacy of intelligence and competence over ignorance, incompetence and debauchery.

Dr. Hoge, pastor of the First Presbyterian Church, who recently preached in the Fifth Avenue Presbyterian Church, New York, and was mentioned as Dr. Hall's successor, took as his text: "He that ruleth his spirit is better than he that taketh a city."

"We have done both," he said. "We have taken a city. That is much, but it is more because it is our own city that we have taken."

Dr. Hoge justified the movement which led to the change of government. [109]

CHAPTER XVII.

At Mrs. McLane's.

It was Thanksgiving Day. The political storm increased tenfold in velocity and destructiveness by race hatred that had swept through the old city of Wilmington, devastating homes, leaving orphans, widows and ruined fortunes in its wake, was slowly abating. A city in a state of siege could not have presented a more distressing appearance. Soldiers and armed white men and boys stood in groups on every street ready to pounce upon and disperse any assemblage of black citizens upon the streets. The ringing of church bells, the call to praise only served to intensify the fear of colored worshippers whose meetings had been previously broken up by armed mobs. These dusky worshippers, devout as they were, had not the faith sufficient to enable them to discern the smiling face of God through the clouds which hung over them. Demoralized, dejected, disconsolate, they dodged about here and there like sheep having no shepherd. Just as the bell in the tall steeple of the old Baptist Church on Market street was making its last long and measured peals there crept out from behind the old Marine Hospital a woman leading a little child by the hand. Both were wretchedly clad. Thrown about the woman's shoulders was an old quilt. Her shoes were tied with strings, which were wrapped around the soles to keep from leaving her feet. Her skirt, tattered and torn, hung dejectedly about her scant form. The child, barefooted and with only one piece to hide its nakedness, dodged behind its mother as it walked to keep the wind from striking with its full force its emaciated body. The woman, though young in years, was old and haggard in face. Her woolly hair, unkempt and sprinkled with gray, the result of just three weeks of privation, apprehension and dread, bulged out from beneath the old shawl which covered her head. At the northwest corner of the hospital fence she paused, looked cheerfully toward her own cottage, but a few blocks away, then slowly [110] walked on in that direction, the child toddling at her side. "What is the bells ringin' for, mamma?" asked the little one. "It ain't Sunday." "It's Thanksgiving Day, and we usually go to church on that day," answered the mother, slowly. "What is Thanksgiving Day?" "It is a day set apart by the President for the people to assemble and give thanks for—for—blessings—received during the year, my child." This last answer tore that disconsolate mother's heart till it bled. She had reached the gate of her cottage, from which she had fled on the night of November 10th to escape insult and murder. A white woman sat upon the steps knitting, her children playing about the yard. The colored woman stood and momentarily gazed in amazement at the intruder upon her premises. "Well, whart du you wannt?" said the white one, looking up from her work and then down again. "What do I want?" returned the colored one. "That's the question for me to ask.

What are you doing in my house?" "Your house?" "Yes, my house!" "Niggers don't own houses in dis here town no mo'; white uns air rulin' now," was the saucy response. "We uns air in these houses, an' we air goin' ter stay in um. An' mo'n thet; them's ther Mair's orders." "You poor white trash; I worked hard for this house, and hold the deed for it, so you get out!" So saying, she caught hold of the latch. The white woman rushed to the corner of the fence and screamed "Police!" at the top of her voice.

"Well, what's ther mater here?" asked one of the four men who came running up in response to the woman's call. "This nigger cums here ter purt me out er this house." "This is my house!" broke in the other. "My house," repeated the man, with a sneer. "Pocession is nine-tents er th' law. She's in, you air out, so git." Several colored people had responded to the call, most of them women. "Come, Eliza," said one, putting her arms affectionately about the wretched and angry woman's waist, while another took the little one in her arms. "It's no use to waste words; we all have suffered at the hands of these superior (?) people. But God will give the wrong-doer his reward in due season. Come with us, my dear, and wait patiently." "All my nice furniture being ruined by this dirty cracker, and I can do nothing to prevent it," sobbed Eliza, struggling to free herself that she might fly at the throat of the intruder, who stood glaring at her in triumph.

"Take her er long," said the white bully, "Or I'll lock her up. The time fer Niggers ter sass white fo'ks is past in Wilmington."

[111] "Come, Eliza; that's a good woman." The woman walked reluctantly away, to be cared for by her neighbors.

That evening at about dusk Mrs. McLane, an old and wealthy white citizen, stood at the window of her palatial dwelling on Third street watching the twilight fade—watching the Thanksgiving Day of 1898 slowly die. Mrs. McLane had not attended church; she felt more like hiding away from the world to be alone with God. In her devotions that morning she had cried out with all the fervency of her soul that God would turn away his anger from a people with whom He was justly displeased.

"My people are to-day imbued with the feeling of boastfulness in their own strength rather than thankfulness to God. For can any of us feel that God has countenanced the murder, pillage and intimidation which the whites of Wilmington have resorted to? And for what?" Thus she soliloquized as she watched the day die. The clock in the old Presbyterian Church slowly chimed the hour of six. A long jingle of the doorbell awoke Mrs. McLane from her reverie. "Mrs. Hill, Mrs. Bruce and Mrs. Engel, missis ," said a servant, slightly pulling the door ajar and pushing her head in. "All right, Margaret, I'll be right down," answered the lady. "Tell Aunt Susan that the guests I expected to tea are here. " "Yes m'm." The servant disappeared, and Mrs. McLane slowly descended to the parlor. "Why, Marjorie!" exclaimed Mrs. Bruce, as the hostess glided into the parlor, where the three women sat chatting. "How could you stay at home from church on such a lovely day! You missed a treat, you—" "Tea's ready, missis," said Margaret, appearing suddenly in the parlor door. "Now, ladies, we must retire to the dining room and let conversation aid digestion; remember that my tea has waited until half an hour past the usual time for you. So, without further delay, let me lead the way to tea," and Mrs. McLane proceeded to the dining room, followed by her three visitors. "Well, from Mrs. Bruce's exclamation when I entered a while ago I must infer that you all enjoyed church service immensely." "Well, I should say so," promptly answered Mrs. Bruce. "I don't see how any one could have remained at home on such a day as this. And, you know, we have so much to be thankful for. Dr. Jose quoted for his text, 'He that is slow to anger is better than the mighty, and he that controlleth his spirit than he that taketh a city.' 'We have taken a city,' said he, 'our city; freed it from [112] ignorance and misrule.' I, for one, am grateful to see our men have so nobly shown to the women of Wilmington that they are worthy of our loyalty and devotion. I said to my husband, after reading that infamous and slanderous article in the Record, that our men were too pigeon-livered to take that Nigger out and give him what he deserves; and I think it was just such talk from our women in the households that brought about this revolution. Such as the white people of Wilmington have been compelled to resort to would never have happened had the good-for-nothing Yankee left the black where he belonged, instead of wrenching him from his master and then educating him into the belief that he is as good as he who owned him. This Manly is a new Nigger—a product of Yankee schools and colleges. Freedom and education have worked only harm to the Negro by putting high notions into his head. Blacks of Wilmington have had more sway than was for their good, and they need checking, and it has come at last. We will have no more black lawyers, doctors, editors and so forth, taking the support from our own professional men. And no more such disgraceful scenes as we have been compelled to endure— well-dressed Negro women flaunting about our streets in finery, when they ought to be in their places. Why, we can't order a gown or bonnet, but what, before we can get into the street with it on our backs, some Nigger woman flirts by with the very same thing on, style, material and all. It is preposterous! How I have burned in desire to jump upon them and tear the things off and flog them, as they deserve. And to go to Seventh street on a Sunday or on a week-day, for that matter, the sight is heart sickening! There Sambo and his woman, dressed to death, strut along with heads erect, looking as important as though they owned the city, or, astride their bicycles, they'll ride plumb over you. But we have put a stop to Nigger high-stepping for a while at least, thanks to our true and patriotic men, blue-blooded Southern gentlemen." "And our boys, who did so nobly!" chimed in Mrs. Engel. "Yes! yes!" exclaimed Mrs. Bruce, with a triumphant laugh. "How full of zeal and love for home and country they are! It was indeed charming to see them hold up big, burly blacks and make them stand until bidden to pass on. One of the most amusing and gratifying sights was the holding up of a big Nigger woman, right in front of my gate. She reared and charged, but to no purpose; those boys made her shake her duds. They pulled her clothes almost off her back trying to make her stand until searched." "And you didn't protest against such [113] ungallant treatment of a woman, and by mere lads?" asked Mrs. McLane. "Protest! Why, Marjorie McLane! You must not, my dear, allow yourself to think of such creatures as women entitled to such consideration as is due white women. How did I know but what that creature had set out to burn some lady's dwelling. Protest? No! decidedly no! I just stood there and enjoyed the fun. I am afraid you are too full of Yankeeism, Marjorie. You should be thankful that our enemies are vanquished. When Colonel Moss reached Dry Pond, instead of showing fight and standing by their editor, whom they upheld in slandering white women, they scampered to the woods." "And the poor frightened creatures are still there. They cannot be induced to return, and the suffering among them is intense. Mothers have given birth out there, and they and their offspring have died from exposure. " "Poor creatures!" exclaimed Mrs. Engel. "God pity them and us!" continued Mrs. McLane. "If what has been done in Wilmington within the last few days is the work of gentlemen, then in the name of God let us have a few men in Wilmington, if such can be found." "But, my dear—" "Don't interrupt me, Mrs. Bruce! Hear me through," said Mrs. McLane, raising her voice. "May the groans of these suffering women and children ever ring in the ears of Colonels Moss and Wade, and may the spirits of their murdered victims unrelentingly pursue them through the regions of hell." "Marjorie McLane!" exclaimed Mrs. Bruce, in astonishment. "Such language from a Southern lady!" said Mrs. Hill. "Yes, a Southern lady clothed in her right mind," returned the hostess. "These men in their blind zeal to restore white supremacy, and to defend women, have unmistakably demonstrated their weakness. White supremacy cannot be maintained by resorting to brute force, neither can the women of one race be protected and defended while the defender of virtue looks upon the destruction of the other race as only an indiscretion.

'Thou must be true thyself
If thou the truth wouldst teach.
Thy soul must overflow
If thou another's soul would reach.'

"Enduring supremacy, the supremacy that will be acknowledged is supremacy of character, supremacy of deportment, supremacy in justice and fair play. We have irreparably lost our hold upon the Negro because we lack these attributes. We must not allow ourselves to feel that the Negro in this enlightened age is incapable of knowing and appreciating true manhood and true [114] gallantry. To shoot men after they have been totally disarmed, and after they have surrendered everything as a peace offering is cowardice without parallel.

"What would Lee and Jackson have said should their departed spirits return to gaze upon men who so bravely followed them through the wilderness, in perilous times, leading in such dastardly work as was done in Wilmington on the 10th of November? 'Whatsoever a man soweth that shall he also reap.' It is not in future fires that men are to get the reward for their doings, but here in this life. Our fathers have sowed the seeds that are sprung up now in race troubles and discord. The North was first to see the danger, and gave the warning; but we blindly plunged into four years of bitter strife, to maintain what we thought was our right. The troubles through which we are passing are the reaping of the fruits of the sowing of our fathers. The conduct of our people on the 10th of November shows plainly to my mind that we are making the same mistakes. We are foolish enough to sow that which will cause the harvester to curse us in his misery. Here were boys not over twelve years of age armed and licensed to insult women, tear their clothes from them and humiliate them. " "Humiliate them!" echoed Mrs. Bruce, with a sneer, "as though such creatures could be humiliated. They are entitled to no respect from white men." "And we should not allow ourselves to think of them as women with the same feelings and propensities that we have," said Mrs. Engel. "I say," continued Mrs. McLane, "that the Negro woman should be considered a woman in the fullest sense of the term, and those men and boys who in their zeal to protect white women humiliated and disgraced black ones, insulted and humbled their own mothers, sisters and sweethearts; for what disgraces one woman disgraces another, be she white, black, red or brown. We, the white people of the South, have acknowledged the black woman's right to all the sympathy that we ourselves may expect. She has carried us in her arms and suckled us at her breast, and in thousands of instances her word has been the only law among our children in our nurseries. She heard and faithfully kept the secrets of our lives. We sought her advice, and believed in the efficacy of her prayers." "Now, Marjorie, you know," said Mrs. Bruce, "that such Negro women are still dear to us; these old mammies and uncles who know and keep in their places are never troubled in the South. The Yankee did us a great injury by lifting the Negro out of his place, and making him feel that he is as good as we are. It is this new Nig [115] ger that is causing all the trouble. The black woman, allowed to dress and flaunt about illures, tempts and often robs our domestic life of its sweetness, while the black man, with the wrong conception of freedom, often makes it impossible for our men to leave their homes unguarded." "Bah! away with such nonsensical babbling! You are saying, Mrs. Bruce, that which down in your innermost soul you do not believe. Such talk as that has given Southern women undesirable notoriety, and is making the world believe that to keep us pure it costs yearly hundreds of ignominious human sacrifices, a thing that we should rise up and brand as a lie! Who is to guard the home of the Negro man? Can we look around Wilmington and believe that his home does not need a stronger arsenal than ours? While we are boiling over with sympathy for Mrs. Hartright, do we think for a moment of the humble home of that Negro father made unhappy by Mr. Hartright? Do we feel pity for Dan Hawes, John Maxim, Charlotte Jones? The Negro no longer feels that the appearance of a white illegitimate among his honestly begotten piccaninnies is an honor bestowed upon his household. Charlotte's case was indeed a sad one. No one knows better than I what a heavy heart she carried after her favorite child, the one she had taken such pains to educate, and from whom she expected so much, fell a victim to the flatteries of a Jew." "Well, must white women stop to lament over such things?" asked Mrs. Hill. "Are we to blame for the shortcomings of these people?" "Yes," answered the hostess. "We have looked on unmoved and beheld our sister in black shorn of all protection by the laws upon the State books of every Southern State, that she may be humiliated with impunity, and we have gloried in her shame."

"Harriet Beecher Stowe's "Uncle Tom's Cabin" is no exaggeration. Simon Legree stalks abroad unrebuked in the South, and Cassies with sad stories of betrayal and humiliation are plentiful." "I do not think it possible to better the black woman morally," said Mrs. Hill. "The germs of high and lofty thought are not in her, that is certain." "Have you ever tried to put that theory to a test?" asked Mrs. McLane sharply. "I cant say that I have," returned Mrs. Hill slowly. "If the Negro is morally low, we are ourselves responsible, and God will call us to account for it. In our greed for gain we stifled every good impulse, fostered and encouraged immorality and unholy living among our slaves by disregarding the sacredness of the marriage relation. 'That which God hath joined together let no man put asunder!' [116] We have done that. We have made a discord in the sweetest music that ever thrilled the human heart—the music of love. I believe that there is that pathos, that true poetry in Negro love-making that no other race possesses. When a child I used to love to listen to the simple and yet pathetic pleading of the Negro boy for the hand of the girl, whom to protect and defend he owned not himself. My very heart would weep when I pictured those fond hearts torn asunder by the slave trader. I could see the boy far away, in some lonely cornfield in Georgia, pause, lean upon his plow and sigh for his lost love as he listened to the cooing of the dove, while she, far away in Tennessee or in some Virginia cornfield mournfully sang as she dropped the yellow corn.
'Ebry time the sun goes down
I hangs ma head an' cries.'
Have we not done enough to a forgiving race? The case of Richard Holmes is a strong proof of the Negroes' high and lofty conception of purity and virtue, and had he been a white man, his actions would have been applauded to the echo. My opinion is that just so long as the safeguards around Negro women are so weak, so long as the laws upon the statute books of Southern States brand her as a harlot, pure or impure, and keep her outside the pale of pity and consideration, just so long will our representatives have to resort to murder and intimidation to get to Congress. The strength of any race rests in the purity of its women, and when the womanhood is degraded, the life blood of a race is sapped. Should we be disappointed under this showing because the Negro does not vote with us? You know as well as I that the Negro's vote was at the bottom of all this trouble. And we will always have trouble as long as the destruction of Negro womanhood is only an indiscretion. Mrs. Fells, of Georgia shows the narrowness of her soul when she cries aloud for the protection of white women in isolated sections of Georgia against lustful Negroes, when she knows perfectly well that Negro girls in Georgia need the same protection against lustful whites. A woman who is not desirous of protecting the innocent of any race is insincere, and should be branded as a hypocrite."

"Mrs. Fells should not be blamed for ignoring Negro women. They are all fallen creatures," said Mrs. Engle. "That's a broad assertion for any woman to make, and there's no white woman that believes it in her innermost soul," returned Mrs. McLane. "The best white blood of the South flows through the veins of Negroes, [117] and this reveals the unmistakable weakness of a superior race. " * * * "The weakness of the men of a superior race! Be careful and make that distinction, Marjorie," said Mrs. Bruce. "Southern white women are the most virtuous women in the world." "That's the general boast," returned Mrs. McLane. "And a boast that cannot be gainsaid," said Mrs. Hill. "Visiting the iniquities of the fathers upon the children to the third and fourth generation," quoted Mrs. McLane slowly. "Do you believe in the truthfulness of God's word?" There was no answer. "You all are willing to admit that the fathers have eaten sour grapes, that the sin of unlawful inter-mixture with the alien is the fault of the men. But can we prove that the taint of lust in the blood of the fathers has come down through the generations to effect the male child only, and leave the female uncontaminated? God has not so ordained it. Our men sin and boast in it. Consorting with the women of the alien race to them is only an indiscretion. While even to acknowledge that in the Negro man are the elements of genuine manhood would make a Southern white women a social exile, and make her the butt of ridicule. Does not this account for the human sacrifices that have shocked the nation? If the Negro's life is cheap and a frank acknowledgement of preference for him means so much to her, and knowing that her word is judge and jury, is it not likely that she would pursue the easiest course? The passing of laws since the war prohibiting the intermarriage of the races is proof that the men do not trust us as implicitly as they pretend. The lynchings and burnings that are daily occurring in the South are intended as warnings to white women as well as checks to Negro men. Men who constitute these mobs care no more for virtue than so many beasts; and saying that they are composed of best citizens does not alter my opinion. Instead of going about as Mrs. Fells is doing, crying for more of the blood of the black men, and vilifying defenseless black women as Mrs. Harris of that same State is doing, we the Southern white women better be doing a little missionary work among the men of our own race. It is time for us to rise up and let our voices be heard against the making of our protection an excuse for crime. Women like Mrs. Harris have done nothing, and would do nothing to better the condition of the woman whom they vilify. Nathan said unto David: 'Thou art the man.' This poor wretch will rise up in the judgment and cry aloud against us as her unnatural sisters who stood upon her and trampled her in the mud and [118] mire. As inferior and morally low as we may deem her, it may be more tolerable for her in the judgment than for us. I wonder sometimes how the black woman could even look with favor upon the man who to her has been and is a sneaking coward, as well as a hypocrite in conduct toward the women of his own race. To us he abuses the Negro women, makes her the subject of ridiculous cartoons, shows her up before the world as a beast with his lips wet with kisses from her mouth, and she suckles at her breast the child of his begetting." "We can't afford to be too plain on that subject, Marjorie," interrupted Mrs. Bruce. "Southern women, not being independent and self-supporting, like our Northern sisters, cannot afford to call the men to account, though we, some of us, see the situation just as you have presented it." "But I for one will speak plainly," said Mrs. McLane. "Officer Bunts, instead of being driven from the city and hung in effigy, should have been treated differently, because in publicly acknowledging that he preferred a Negro woman as a companion he showed that he was more of a man than those who, like the Pharisees, rose up against him. If we as parents should refuse to give our daughters in marriage to men who have not clandestinely consorted with women of the alien race, how many could hold up clean hands?"

"She who comes through environments of temptation unprotected from the assaults of the devil to glory and immortality will have a more exceeding and eternal weight of glory than she who has been shut in, as it were, by the walls of a nunnery." "If we could have kept the Negro from the Bible, kept the religion of Jesus Christ out of his heart, the massacre of November 10th might have the effect that those who planned it desired. But such demonstrations of barbarism will never be the means of vanquishing a trusting people. There's my cook, Susan. Her faith is simply astonishing. That young Negro man who was shot to death trying to escape from the Naval Reserves who were taking him from his home and family was her son. When my son read the news to her, she said no word, there was no sign of distress in her face, but I could see that her heart was deeply moved. She arose after a few minutes' silent meditation, then went on with her work. That evening I stole up to her room to speak a comforting word to her. I found her reading her Bible. She took off her glasses and wiped the water from her eyes as I entered." "I'm jes' layin' hold of God's promises," she said with a smile. "God is our refuge an' strength in all kinds [119] er trouble, Honey." She threw her arms about my neck and drew me down beside her, and pointing to a verse in the prayer of Habakkuk said: "Read it loud, Honey. That's whar I stan'. 'Although the fig tree shall not blossom, neither shall fruit be in the vines, the labor of the olive shall fail, and the fields shall yield no meat.' 'The flock shall be cut off from the fold and there shall be no herd in the stalls. Yet will I rejoice in the Lord, I will joy in the God of my salvation.' These are her sentiments." "This demonstrates the strength of her faith. She will not believe that her child was killed. In some miraculous way he must have escaped, and will some day come to her. For the faith of the simple Negro woman I would give a world." It was near the midnight hour when Mrs. McLane's visitors departed, wiser women by that Thanksgiving Day visit, we hope. [120]

CHAPTER XVIII.

The Colonel's Repentance.

The riotous excitement was slowly abating in the old city. The woods were full of panic-stricken, starving colored people, and trains were leaving the city laden with those who had means to get away. The leading whites, feeling both alarmed at and ashamed of the havoc and misery their ambition had wrought, had begun to send men into the woods to carry food to the starving, and induce them to return to the city. But so thoroughly frightened were these poor refugees that the sight of white faces made them run away from the very food offered them. The ambassadors came back to the city disgusted, and dispatched colored men, who were more successful. It was the evening of the 15th of November. Mr. Julius Kahn, Eastern North Carolina's representative of the Life Insurance Company of Virginia, sat at his desk in his office on Front street. This company, which had been giving, for a small weekly payment, quite a substantial and satisfactory death benefit, and consequently doing quite an enormous business among the poorer classes of the colored people, were among the heaviest sufferers from the massacre, for some of the collectors had been pressed into the service of the rioters to shoot down, and intimidate their very means of support. As Mr. Kahn sat there, he saw nothing but absolute ruin staring him in the face. "Well, what news?" he asked a man who stalked in, and sank heavily into a chair. The man threw his book upon the desk before him, shrugged his shoulders and sighed wearily. "It's useless," he answered finally. "I give it up. I haven't succeeded in getting within ten yards of a nigger woman to-day. If I went in at the front door, every occupant in a house would bolt out at the back one, and run for dear life. They will listen to no overtures of friendship. Our very faces fill them with abject terror. We had just as well throw up the insurance business and quit, as far as Wilmington is concerned. God's curse on the men who are responsible for this [121] blight upon the good name of this city. One woman opened her door, cursed me, threw her book at me, and slammed the door in my face; and I can't blame her, for she saw and recognized me among the mob who shot her husband down right in her gate. And God knows I did not want to be among them, but was compelled to. And they say that old devil, after usurping the Mayoralty of the city, and killing and driving from their homes so many colored people, has softened, and has sent out to induce the wretches to return," said Mr. Kahn after a long pause. "Yes," returned the agent, "but that won't help us. They say they've lost their confidence in white people. Why, you have no idea what a wretched state of things I've come across. The last five days' experience has made raving maniacs out of some of the niggers. The papers have announced the giving out of rations at the City Hall to-morrow, but I doubt if many will go to get them." Mr. Kahn leaned over, rested his elbows upon the desk, and slowly ran his fingers through his hair. "Some of our men left the city before they would be mixed up in this affair, and I wish now that I had done the same. But," he continued slowly, "we may just as well wait until all excitement is at an end before we pull up stakes. Other blacks will doubtless pour in to fill the places of those that are going, and we may be enabled to build up business." "You can remain and wait, Mr. Kahn," answered the agent rising. "This accursed town can no longer hold me. I leave to-night for Richmond, for I can no longer look into the faces of the people whom I have had a hand in killing and terrorizing. Good bye, Mr. Kahn," and the collector was gone.

"Everybody git in line an' pass one ba one before ther Mair an' git yer permits; fer yer can't git rations thoughten 'um," shouted a policeman to a crowd of hungry citizens who stood upon the steps of the City Hall. "Git in thur ole Aunty an' wait yer turn!" to an old lady, who started to leisurely climb the steps. The Mayor sat at his desk, which had been placed just behind the railing in the court room, and mildly lectured each applicant as he or she came up. "This state of affairs is terrible, but it's your own fault. White people were born to rule, and you to obey. We liberated you and we can re-enslave you. Freedom and Yankee advice have ruined a good many of you. What's your name, old Aunty?" he asked an old woman who came limping up. "Maria Tapp'n, marster," answered the old woman courte [122] sing. "That's right, you haven't lost your manners," said the Mayor with a smile, writing out for her an order for a double portion. "Emulate these old mammies and uncles, who know their places, and you will have no trouble. Next!" "Ef ther's eny who needs er double po'tion hits ther widders an' orphans," said a policeman gently, pushing a little woman in black before the Mayor's desk. "Whose widow are you?" asked the Mayor. "Was your husband killed in the riots?—resisting arrest, I suppose." "This is ther widder of Dan Wright," answered the policeman; "an' ef Wilmin'ton had er had a hundred niggers like that, we uns would er had er diff'ant tale ter tell. He was ded game." "Dan Wright," repeated the Mayor slowly. "He's ther darkey that drawed er bead on an' defied we uns ter the las'," said the policeman pushing the woman away, and pushing another up to the desk. But the Mayor neither answered nor looked up. One by one they continued to come up to receive their orders and pass out; but the executive looked them no more in the face, nor essayed to speak. The crowd slowly dwindled away until the last applicant had passed out. The Mayor laid his pen upon the desk before him, leaned back in his chair, raised his feet upon the desk, and fell into a reverie. The doings of the past few days came back to his mind in all their shocking significance. The curses, the groans, the agonizing cries of the bereaved and the dying sounded a hundred-fold more voluminous and heart-rending. Then the bloody form of Dan Wright appeared with hands uplifted, eyes staring at his murderers, the blood streaming from a hundred wounds.

The Mayor had seen hard service in war, was one of the immortal few who, under the leadership of Pickett, made that gallant but futile charge at Gettysburg, to be driven back for a third time, crushed, mangled and defeated. He doubtless assisted in digging the trenches into which those ghastly remnants that told of the cannon's awful work were thrown. That was war, and such sights had never so affected the veteran as the vision now before him.

"Avaunt! avaunt! Quit my sight!
Let the earth hide thee!
Thy bones are marrowless, thy blood is cold;
Thou hast no speculation
In those eyes that thou dost glare with!"

The Mayor started up, opened his eyes. Uncle Guy stood before him. "I jes' taut I'd drap in, Kurnel, but didn't speck ter [123] fin' yer sleep," said he, wincing under the Mayor's abstracted gaze. "Oh, I don' want nut'n; don' make er scratch on dat paper. I ain't beggin'," he exclaimed, as the Mayor, recovering, reached for his pen. "That's so Guy; you needn't be a beggar as long as the white people own a crust," he answered, settling back in his chair again. "Well, what are Negroes saying about the uprising, Guy?" The old man shrugged his shoulders, and shook his index finger at the Mayor. "Le' me tell yo', Kurnel, you na Wilmin'ton rich bocra, dun throw yo' number an' los'; hear me? Ef enybody gone tell me dat dese people I bin raise wid, who bin called de bes' bocra in de worl' would go an' kick up all dis ere devil, I'd er tole um No." The old man straightened up, pointed skyward. "Lowd deliver yunna bocra when yer call befo' de bar. Dese niggers ain't su'prise at po' white trash; dey do enyting. But yunna fus class white fo'ks—"

"Well, Guy," broke in the Mayor, "it was hard for us to resort to such, but it was in self-defense." "Self-defense! self-defense!" repeated the old man. "When po' nigger han bin tie, an' yunna bocra got eberyt'ing—gun, cannon an' all de am-nition, an' beside dat, de town full wid strange trash frum all ober de country to crush dem? Some er dese men I sees shootin' an' killin', dars men an' umen livin' er my race dat nussed an' tuk keer er dem w'en dey bin little. God er mighty gwinter pay yunna well fer yer work, Kurnel, an' de gost er dem po' murdered creeters gwine ter haunt yo' in yer sleep. God don' lub ugly, an' yunna can't prosper." The old man concluded with a low bow, strode out, and left the Mayor alone with his thoughts. [124]

CHAPTER XIX.

Teck Pervis, the Leader.

"Come, stan' back, men! I led you uns this fer, an' kin lead you through. I'm goin' ter lead the way ter ther Mare's office. Foller me!" A crowd of disappointed poor whites, who had assisted in restoring white supremacy and who had not been treated fairly in the distribution of the spoils, had gathered upon the City Hall steps in Wilmington to state their grievances and have them adjusted. Teck Pervis, the chairman of White Supremacy League of Dry Pond and leader of the raiders on the 10th of November, pushed his way through the crowd and faced the Mayor, who, seeing them approaching, had sent forward a platoon of police to intercept them, but without effect. "I say, Mr. Mare," said the leader, fumbling with his hat, "we uns heard that you sont orders fer us ter turn in our guns." "I did give such orders," returned the Mayor calmly. "Le' me tell yer, Mr. Mare, you uns ain't filled yer contract wid we po' uns, an' ther hain't er goin' ter be eny turnin' in guns tell yer do." "State your grievance," commanded the Mayor, in a tone that betrayed the ugliness of his temper. "You hain't carried out yer promus by a jug full," said Teck. "We uns have ter have ther pintin' er half er ther new officers in ther city. We uns war ter be giv'n these big-bug niggers' houses, churches an' so on. Niggers places in ther sto'es an' every whar was ter be giv' ter we uns. Now, drot my hides, ef these things air takin' shape zactly ter suit we uns. Now, we want satisfaction." "Well," said the Mayor, "we thank you gentlemen for your zeal in helping us to rid Wilmington of radical rule, but we are sorry that you misunderstood us in regard to spoils and so forth. We can't take from the Negro his property and give it to you, but in cases where he has been timid enough to give it up (and we have had instances of the kind) we have sustained the white man. As many of the merchants as could consistently do so have discharged their black [125] help and put on whites. But complaints are coming in to me that you can't do their work; that it often takes two white men to perform one Negro's task. Good and reliable colored help are leaving the city in alarming numbers, and we must call a halt. Mr. Skidmore tells me that he tried a few whites at his mill a few days ago and the result was most unsatisfactory. They couldn't count and pile the lumber and run the saws, and the scheme is a dead loss. What are we to do? We have given you the street work, and the police force is full. You men are not sufficiently educated to fill clerical positions, and even if you were, we must reserve them for the first families," concluded the Mayor, with a haughty lift of his head. "Now, Mr. Mare, yo' speech is all right 'nough, but it don't suit we uns ernough ter give up ther guns. We went back on our colored frends ter giv' yo' 'ristocrats ther gov'ment, and we uns'll combine wi' ther colored men an' take hit from yer, see?"

Teck Pervis turned and faced the men who stood like a wall at his back. "Gentermen, go home an' keep yer guns an' yer powder dry, for yo'll need 'em! Good day, Mr. Mare!" He followed and addressed his men from the steps of the City Hall.

"Gentermen, we pu' down nigger rule on the tenth, the nex' move mus' be ter let ther 'ristocrats know thet the one gullus boys air indowed by God wi' ther same rites as they air. We po' uns'll have er show, er break up the whole thing. Go home, boys, and be ready to rally when ther order's giv'!"
[126]

CHAPTER XX.

Rev. Jonas Melvin, Resigns.

"I've bin er readin' ther Scripter an' rastlin' wi' ther Lord in prayer fer lo these meny ye'rs, an' hain't never seed er time when I tho't thet er preacher of ther word was jestified in j'inin' in with sinners in devilment. Thar's no use in talkin', Brother Melvin mus' wine up his kareer in Free Will Church." Mrs. Aamanda Pervis was addressing the above to Deacon Littleton, as arm in arm they proceeded toward the church a few evenings after Thanksgiving Day. Ever since the massacre she had been busily trying to awaken sentiment in the church against the pastor, who on that fatal day had stood with Dr. Jose upon the firing line to shoot down his fellow citizens of color. The deacons had waited upon Jonas Melvin and informed him of what was being done, and had advised him to tender his resignation and get out; but he preferred coming before the church and "quitting honorably," as he termed it. Mrs. Pervis had worked so earnestly that the church was crowded to the doors on that evening. It was Deacon Littleton who called the meeting to order and stated its purpose. "Brethren an' sisters," he began, "the 10th of November was to the people of this community a tryin' time. It was a war which many of us felt justifiable in enterin', but there was no justification in it; it was the work of the devil. If we had got on our knees an' kept our eyes fixed upon the things of God, such a deed as has disgraced this community would not have happened. I wonder what the Negro thinks of us now? Does he think we air the banner carriers of Christian civilization? Orphans are cryin', widows are moanin', a paradise has been turned into hell by a people calling themselves a superior people. Christians and sinners have gone hand and hand into this evil. We don't know whether any other church has felt in duty boun' to sift its membership, an' reprimanded the guilty, but Free Will Baptist Church feels it her indispensable duty to do so, an' we are sorry to say that the first case we are pained to [127] try is that of our pastor, Rev. Jonas Melvin, who, on the 10th of November, 1898, stood with gun in hand, assisting the devil in his work." Turning to the minister, who sat all the while with head bowed, the deacon concluded: "Brother Jonas Melvin, have you anything to say to this charge, why it should not be sustained, and you be dismissed from this church?"

Rev. Jonas Melvin arose. "Brethren," he began, "this work began in the church; church people laid the plans and led in the execution of those plans. Those men who waited upon the Governor to persuade him to keep the troops away that the mob might execute its work unmolested, were leading church men and ministers of the gospel." "They were no Christians!" cried a feminine voice. "I thought I was doing my duty as a Christian in assisting in restoring good government to the people of this town, and if I have done wrong, the Lord is my judge." Mr. Melvin sat down. "The state of things as they existed in Wilmington did not justify the taking of a single life," said a brother, rising, "and many a man has been made to stumble by the deeds of professing Christians in this riot; and while I'm on my feet, I move that the resignation of Rev. Jonas Melvin from the pastorate of this church be demanded." "Secon' ther motion!" exclaimed Mrs. Pervis, jumping to her feet. "An' I wish ter say jes' here that Teck Pervis, who perfessed religion las' year, has jes' gone back to ther deval bekase, ses he, the preachers war in this thing. Preachers whose han's air full er blood air not fit ter handle ther word er God."

The motion was carried with but few opposers. Mrs. Pervis felt light enough to fly away that night as she walked homeward, for she had carried the church with her for God and the right. She hugged the arm of Deacon Littleton with painful tenacity as they both strode homeward together. "Think of them po' creeters drove frum ther homes ter suffer an' die by men claimin' ter hev religion. Jonas Melvin mus' go back ter Georgy whar the people air in leeg wid ther deval."
[128]

CHAPTER XXI.

Bill Sikes.

Bill Sikes was a man who always looked ahead and wisely prepared for declining years. Bill was a carpenter by trade, and by thrift and industry saved money, bought land and built houses upon it, so that he might leave comfortable homes for his many children. When the calamity came which incapacitated him for further usefulness he had come into possession of a whole block in the portion of the city known as "New Town." His prosperity did not, however, lessen his activity; he forgot that he was getting old, for his limbs were yet supple and his eyes perfectly clear. He measured off his lumber and drove nails with the strength and accuracy of a young man; yet, as death lurks in every passing breeze, feeling well is no evidence of sound health or assurance of long life. Bill Sikes seldom complained. Steady habits had made him vigorous and confident; but one morning his fond wife stood in the door and watched him as with head erect and firm step he strode away to his work, only to be borne back to her at noon a helpless paralytic. "What's the matter, William?" she asked tenderly, as loving hands lay him upon the lounge before her. But the tongue which had bid her good-bye so fondly that morning could not utter a word, and the eyes that had gazed so sweetly into hers bespoke the bitter anguish of his soul as they stared vacantly at her. "He's done fer," said one of the men, rubbing his eye with the back of his hand. "The doctors seen him and says he ain't fer long." "Speak to me, William," cried Mrs. Sikes, bending low and pressing her cheeks against her husband's. He raised his arm to caress her, but it fell again to his side.

But Bill Sikes did not die; he rallied; the lost strength gradually came back to his palsied limbs sufficiently to enable him to hobble around, and his tongue became light enough to utter words that could be understood with difficulty. Full and complete [129] recovery was impossible, however; he was a child, helplessly clinging to his wife, whose burden was increased tenfold with the larger children all away and management of everything—the looking after their little store and other property upon her shoulders; she felt that God had tried her as no other soul had been tried. The property of Bill Sikes had for a long time been coveted by his white neighbors, but even extortionate offers had been refused. But the 10th of November offered a favorable opportunity for the covetous to bulldoze black men who owned valuable real estate into selling it at any price, and Mrs. Sikes was one of that number whose experience had turned their love for the dear old home into hate. She had witnessed the killing of a poor wretch right in front of her door, within a stone's throw of his home; had heard the agonizing wails of his wife and children—a sight which she had never expected to witness in Wilmington. The roar of cannon and musketry, the yells of frightened women and children kept her poor, helpless husband in constant terror, hanging on to her skirts like a babe. And now, although weeks had passed since that fatal day, the native white, emboldened by re-enforcement and the demoralization of colored men, kept up the reign of terror. Colored women of respectability who had not fled the city were compelled to remain prisoners in their homes to escape ignominious treatment upon the highways.

It was a few mornings after Thanksgiving Day when Mrs. West left her cottage on Campbell street and ventured over to pay a visit to Mrs. Sikes. "Well, Henrietta, how have you managed to live through it all?" she asked, throwing her arms about the waist of Mrs. Sikes, who saw her approaching, and had gone out upon the porch to greet her. "And poor William! I've thought of you oh! so many times, Henrietta, knowing of just how much you were in need of his protection during these days of trial." "Yes," answered Mrs. Sikes, leading the visitor in and bolting the door. "The burden upon his poor wife's shoulders is indeed heavy; but, then, our men are unable to protect us, anyway, so great are the odds against them." "Oh, Wilmington! Wilmington! who would have thought that thou wouldst be the theatre for the tragedy enacted within thy borders!" interrupted Mrs. West. "Some of us, at least, are too well bred, have too much self-respect and pride to stand and endure this state of things that exists now in our home. We could go to church and worship unmolested in the days of slavery; now we have not been permitted for weeks to hold public worship. They are determined to place and keep [130] North Carolina on a level with States further South. Would you believe it? one of our white ladies sent her servant down to the bandit Mayor to be whipped the other day." "Yes," said Mrs. Sikes, "another went down to have a Negro woman driven out of her own house because she lived in a white neighborhood and the children had had a little trouble among themselves. And the poor black woman, to remain in her house, was compelled to get down on her knees and beg the white one's pardon." "Well," said Mrs. West, "we held a meeting the other night, and I told the few who had the courage to venture out that I was going. Give me liberty or give me death! I would rather be a beggar in a land of liberty than a Croesus where my wealth will not purchase toleration. The colored citizens who own property are the very ones who have been forced to leave the city." "I have also made up my mind to do the same," answered Mrs. Sikes. "William is so disgusted that he wants to go even if he has to sell our property for half its value. Then he thinks that in New York he can go under treatment in one of the many great hospitals there. He has improved so much that he believes final recovery possible. To tell you the truth, I did not believe that I could become so disgusted with my own home, in which I was born and loved so well." "It may all be for the best," said Mrs. West. "Some one hath sinned—there is an Achan in the camp, and when the sin is punished innocent and guilty suffer alike. In our prosperity we have strayed away from Him who hath redeemed us, and these broken down aristocrats and poor white indentured slaves are the Philistines sent to scourge us. And, then, we have been slaves to the idea that there is no place on earth for us to live but here in our home. The eagle hath stirred up her nest that her young may scatter abroad. Old as I am, I will leave Wilmington, trusting in God and feeling that the world is mine, and if I can't live in peace in one place I can go to another. But the most important thing is, Molly has consented to go." "Brave girl!" said Mrs. Sikes. "I heard of her wonderful deeds during the massacre; I didn't believe it was in her. In her new surroundings, away from old associate, she will keep straight. I have made up my mind to go finally to Cleveland, Ohio, my old home. Colored women are not so much annoyed by white men in the North and West as in the South, and Molly may there be enabled to quit her old habits. We will see each other before we start away, as I shall take a steamer, for we may stay a while in New York," concluded Mrs. West, rising to go. "It matters not where on earth [131] we may roam, there are twelve gates to the City up there. There is no more parting, no more persecution, no more separation, no tears. So long, till I see you again."

The usurping Mayor of Wilmington had just disposed of the last case upon docket, dismissed the court and had settled back in his chair to enjoy the morning paper, when Bill Sikes entered, and, with his hat in his hand, humbly approached the railing behind which the Mayor sat. He rested his palsied hand upon the rail and saluted. The Mayor arose, came forward and extended his hand. "Well, Bill, how are you?" "Mornin', Colonel," answered he. "I come down to tell yer I'm goin'." "Going? Where?" "I think I'll try the North, Colonel." The Mayor's face relaxed. "Why, Bill, you are all right; no one's troubled you. If all the Negroes were like you we would have had no trouble." "Yes, I know I'm all right," answered Bill, "but I can't stan' seein' men who was playmates of mine shot down on the streets like dogs by their ol' 'sociates an' neighbors. You know, Colonel, I'm one who b'lieved in the white people of this town, an' was ready at any time to stake ma life on that belief; but what has took place in Wilmington an' what is still goin' on has converted me." "Now, Bill," said the Mayor, somewhat moved, "the white people of Wilmington had to resort to this to restore the government to those to whom it rightfully belonged. White people must rule, Bill." "I ain't got no objection to your rulin', but drivin' out black citizens who have stood by yer an' been always faithful to yer is er grave mistake. The deal yer made with these po-bocra is goin' ter give yer trouble, Colonel, mark ma words. You ain't got no more use fer po' whites than I have, an' I know it." "But they were the means to the end, Bill," answered the Mayor, with a smile. "A kingdom divided agin itself is er goin' ter fall, Colonel." "Don't be a fool and leave your home because of unpleasantness; remember you are getting old; the North is no place for you; you are comfortably fixed here." "Yes, Colonel, I know that, but I'm not goin' ter stay in er place where a d—n scoundrel can insult ma wife an' I can't pertect her, an' you know there's been a time when I could. Good-bye, Colonel." "Good-bye, Bill; you'll regret it I'm afraid."

Bill Sikes went back home to prepare for his journey northward.
[132]

CHAPTER XXII.

A Ship Sails.

When on the evening of December 1, 1898, the old Clyde steamer drifted out from her docks into mid stream in the harbor of Wilmington, among the host of passengers that stood upon her deck, with tear-dimmed eyes, to bid adieu to the dear old town was Molly Pierrepont. Leaning upon the shoulder of her foster mother, whose heart was too full to speak, she frantically waved her handkerchief and cried "Farewell, old home! Dear as thou hast been to me, I must leave thee for ever; for thou art in the possession of the wicked. The spoiler is in thy borders. The blood of innocents has flowed freely in thy highways, and the murderer and the assassin stalk abroad in thy streets. But it matters not where I go, thy days of equity, when every citizen, it mattered not how humble, was free, shall ever live with me. Days of childhood innocence, the

shouts of the children, the clang of the school bell, the rippling of the rills, the hum of bees will be the means of helping me to forget thy latter days of turmoil and strife. Good-bye, old home! Good-bye!"
[133]

CHAPTER XXIII.

Bill Sikes in New York.

It was near the Christmas holidays, a genuine Northern winter day, cold and piercing, going to the marrow in spite of heavy clothing. Francis Lewis, contractor and builder, sat in his comfortable office in West Forty-seventh street, New York city, when the door was pushed open and a light-skinned colored man entered. His face was thin and pinched, his hair and beard slightly mixed with gray, and he dragged one foot as he walked.

"Well, what can I do for you, my good man?" said Mr. Lewis, rising. "Take a seat; you don't look as though you are very well," pointing to a chair near by. "I'm jes' lookin' aroun'," answered the man, lowering himself into the chair with difficulty. "I'm er carp'nter maself." "Yes? Where are you from?" asked Mr. Lewis. "From the South—Wilmington," was the reply. "Oh, that's the scene of recent riots. What's the matter with those people down there—crazy?" "No, but that was the only way they could git er hol' er the gov'nment," answered the colored man. "The colored people bein' in the majority of course had controlin' power, but they were always willin' fer the whites ter rule, an' they did rule. But there wasn't offices ernough to go 'round to all the bankrup' whites who wanted political jobs, and give the Negro er repersentation too, so they concluded ter wipe the Negro off the earth." "Shame! shame!" exclaimed Mr. Lewis. "Then the colored people were gittin' er lon too well; they had considerable property, and was well up in the trades an' professions. I owned er whole block maself, an' was perpared to spen' ther balance of ma days at ease, but had ter sell ma house an' git out." "You say you are a carpenter—house builder?" "Yes, sir." "You mean to say that you took contracts, planned and built houses?" "Oh, yes," replied the colored man. "I never saw a colored architect. Say, George!" to a man who had just entered, "here's a colored architect and house-builder from the South." "Architect and builder?" queried the other, [134] drawing nigh. "Well, Mr.—what is your name?" "William—William Sikes." "Mr. Sikes, are you looking for work at your trade in the North? The Trades Union and so forth make it pretty hard for a colored man to get in here; and then you can't work, you are lame." "I am a little lame," replied Bill, looking down at his palsied arm. "I had a paralytic stroke some time er go. I am goin' in for treatment, an' if I git well, I won't ask Trade Union an' labor unions no boot. Where there's er will there's er way." "But I am afraid you will never recover sufficient strength to work again at your trade, my man," answered Mr. Lewis, tenderly; "but you can try. " "Good day," said Bill, rising to go. "Good day," said Mr. Lewis.

But Mrs. Sikes, still vigorous and strong, found in New York abundant opportunities for women to be useful. There was day's work, general house work, chamber work and cooking situations to be had without very much effort on the part of the seeker. Mrs. Sikes, whose work had chiefly been dressmaking and plain sewing, found the new field of labor quite irksome. The money realized from the sale of her property she must not let dwindle away too swiftly; her husband was helpless, and she must work, and the children must work. She found the North a place where a day's work meant a day's work in full; there was no let up; the pound of flesh was exacted. So she often tugged home to her apartments very tired and discouraged.

They had been in New York quite a year, and Mrs. Sikes had quite gotten used to Northern ways (everything seeming easier accomplished), when one evening at the dinner table she noticed that her husband watched her more than usual. "What's the matter, William?" she asked, tenderly. "I'm awful discouraged," he said. "I—I don't get any better, an' hate ter see you an' children strugglin' so hard an' I can't help." "Now, don't worry about that, William; it will do no good." "I was thinkin'," he went on, "that we might try it again in Wil—" "Now, don't mention Wilmington to me again, William!" broke in Mrs Sikes, sharply. "If you wish to go back to that hell, I'll put you on the train and you can go; but I, never! Life is not so easy here, but I can walk the streets as a lady, and my children are free to play and romp without fear of being killed for accidentally or purposely treading upon the toe of a white child. I have been free too long to endure slavery for one moment. Wilmington is not what it used to be, and I fear it never will be. I have just received a letter from Mrs. Cole saying that the situation has not [135] changed. On Castle street about a month ago a black child's body was found full of bruises. It is supposed he was killed by white boys in sport. A young man was called to his door a few nights ago and shot down because he had driven his horse over a gentleman's (?) dog. She says to appeal to the law is useless. She says further that the poor whites are preparing for another raid. Now, I would rather live here free in poverty than to live there a slave in comfort. The children are all away, the property is sold, and there is nothing to be gained by going." Bill said no more to his wife upon the subject; he knew her too well to misunderstand her words.
[136]

Molly's Final Step.

It was Sunday evening in New York. Bethel Church was crowded to the doors. The sermon had been concluded, and the choir and congregation had solemnly chanted the Lord's Prayer. "As I looked over this audience to-night," said Dr. Henderson, descending from the pulpit, "I think of the words of the blessed Saviour, 'The fields are white and ready to harvest,' so I'm going to open the doors of the church. Who here is ready to make a start for heaven to-night? Come, sinner! God's not calling the righteous, but you. There is a prodigal child here to-night who has wandered from home. Come home; there is bread and to spare, and a warm welcome there. Here comes one, thank God!" A young man went forward and took the minister's hand, followed by two others. "Who else will come? There is some one that is almost persuaded. Remember that to be almost persuaded is to be lost. Come, sinner.

"'Will you scorn the message
Sent in mercy from above?
Every sentence, oh how tender!
Every line is full of love.'

"Listen to it: 'Every line is full of love.' God requires no preparation; come just as you are. Just surrender yourself, yourself to—" "I surrender, Lord." This exclamation startled the audience, and all eyes were turned upon a tall and stately woman, who suddenly arose in the centre of the church and started forward. This was Molly Pierrepont, making the final step. "Poor Magdalene," she whispered as she took Dr. Henderson's hand. "But God is gracious, my child," returned the minister.

A month went by. It was Sunday evening, and again Bethel was filled to overflowing; but, large as that audience was, a serene stillness prevailed, for out from the choir loft a rich soprano voice, pathetic and appealing in its tone, fell serenely upon listening ears.
"Just as I am thou wilt receive,
Wilt welcome, pardon, cleanse, relieve;
Because thy promise I believe
Oh Lamb of God, I come.
"Just as I am, thy love unknown,
Hath broken every barrier down,
Now to be Thine, yea Thine alone,
Oh Lamb of God, I come."
Molly has done her part nobly and well, so I close the story with Molly.

Transcriber's note

The following changes have been made to the text:

Page 4: "Whose there" changed to " Who's there".

Page 13: "State from mountian" changed to "State from mountain ".

Page 21: "Good da , Gideon" changed to "Good day, Gideon".

Page 25: "Georgia and Florida its" changed to "Georgia and Florida it's ".

Page 29: "Kidder s Hill" changed to " Kidder's Hill".

Page 35: "anti-bellum liking" changed to " ante-bellum liking".

Page 44: "the main thorougfare" changed to "the main thoroughfare ".

Page 44: "by offering to puschase" changed to "by offering to purchase ".

Page 59: "it is writeen" changed to "it is written ".

Page 63: "great' eal" changed to " great 'eal ".

Page 92: " Wilmington Record " was italicized.

Page 93: "Dr. Pond" changed to " Dry Pond".

Page 111: "Misses," said a servant" changed to " missis ," said a servant".

Page 113: "Such langauge" changed to "Such language ".

Page 134: "make it prety hard" changed to "make it pretty hard".

***